D1454204

PEOPLE MANAGEMENT AND DEVELOPMENT

CIPD REVISION GUIDE 2005

DAVID FARNHAM
PAUL SMITH

Chartered Institute of Personnel and Development

Published by the Chartered Institute of Personnel and Development,
CIPD House, Camp Road, London, SW19 4UX

First published 2005

Design and typesetting by Curran Publishing Services, Norwich
Printed in Great Britain by The Cromwell Press, Trowbridge, Wiltshire

British Library Cataloguing in Publication Data
A catalogue record of this revision guide is available from the
British Library

ISBN 1 84398 080 0

The views expressed in this manual are the authors' own and may not
necessarily reflect those of the CIPD.

The CIPD has made every effort to trace and acknowledge copyright
holders. If any source has been overlooked, CIPD Enterprises would be
pleased to redress this for future editions.

Chartered Institute of Personnel and Development, CIPD House,
Camp Road, London, SW19 4UX
Tel: 020 8971 9000   Fax: 020 8263 3333
Email: cipd@cipd.co.uk   Website: www.cipd.co.uk
Incorporated by Royal Charter. Registered Charity No. 1079797

CONTENTS

PREFACE

The purpose of this CIPD revision guide is to prepare students for the examination that covers the People Management and Development (PM&D) Standard of the Institute. It outlines the relevant content and guides students through the revision and examination process. Although it is particularly aimed at students preparing for the CIPD's own examinations at externally assessed centres, its coverage of the PM&D syllabus and on examination technique more generally makes it also of relevance for those at internally assessed centres.

People Management and Development is a compulsory core for all candidates. It forms the spine of the entire Professional Development Scheme and CIPD Standards. Its aim is to cover the essential knowledge and understanding which is then developed and extended in the other standards.

The authors, Professor David Farnham, Chief Examiner PM&D, and Paul Smith, Senior Lecturer at the University of Hertfordshire, offer advice to students on how to apply the learning acquired during their course of study so as to pass the examination. The authors have extensive experience of both teaching and examining in this field of study at postgraduate level and are thus able to write from this dual perspective.

This CIPD revision guide takes account of the fact that CIPD students often study on a part-time rather than a full-time basis. Part-time professional study is often combined with employment as well as a variety of other activities. This guide is therefore aimed at those individuals whose time is likely to be limited and at a premium.

This guide to examination preparation and revision is designed to be used in conjunction with the core text *People management and development* by Marchington and Wilkinson (2002), and reference is made to this text at appropriate points. Students should also be prepared to supplement this with additional reading, as well as keeping up to date with developments in the field, and advice is given on how best to do this.

Section 1, Chapter 1 of the guide outlines the key content of the PM&D Standard, thus enabling students to identify what needs to be covered during a course of study and what needs to be subsequently revised. Students should familiarise themselves with this content as early as possible in their studies. Examples of past examination questions are given to illustrate the standards.

Section 2 provides advice on how to tackle revision and the examination.

Chapter 2 offers guidance on studying and time management, as well as on how to ensure that revision is carried out in a focused and structured manner. Students who have already read a revision guide for other subjects in this series may find that certain parts of this chapter are similar and can thus be skim-read.

In Chapter 3, the CIPD chief examiner offers insights into the May 2004 PM&D examination. A commentary is provided as to what the expectations of the examination were, and how each question was tackled by students.

Section 3 covers examination practice and feedback.

Chapter 4 provides examples of some of the responses given to questions in the May 2004 examination paper. These are taken from different sources and provide an indication of the standard needed to achieve a pass level in this examination. A selection of questions from previous examinations is also outlined, together with guidance as to expectations. As part of their revision, it is suggested that students try out questions themselves. They can then compare their responses with the ones suggested in the chapter.

We hope that you enjoy your studies and we wish you good luck in the examination. By following the guidance presented here, you should be able to gain the maximum benefit when preparing for, revising and taking the PM&D examination.

David Farnham and Paul Smith
July 2004

SECTION 1

CIPD PROFESSIONAL STANDARDS

1 CIPD PROFESSIONAL STANDARDS

Introduction

The purpose of this chapter is first to introduce the concepts and competencies that underpin the CIPD's Professional Standards, and second to outline the specific People Management and Development (PM&D) Standard. This will enable students to ascertain what needs to be revised in order to cover the standard appropriately in preparation for the examination.

The CIPD's new revised Professional Standards were produced in 2001 after a two-year consultation period. They aim to incorporate developments in the practice of people management, and in the thinking that underlies these, since the previous standards were introduced.

The standards are an articulation of the knowledge and competence required to undertake a professional personnel or training and development role. They aim to define 'What is a CIPD professional?' The Institute has defined standards across the whole spectrum of personnel and development, taking into account both specialist and generalist functions.

The PM&D examination tests students against the Institute's revised Professional Standard for that field. Students need to be familiar with this standard.

Key concepts and competencies

A number of key concepts underpin the CIPD's Standards.

The first concept is that of the 'thinking performer'. In essence, those who fulfil the standards must be capable of thinking, at both an operational and strategic level, and they must be able to put this into practice in performing at the business unit level.

CIPD candidates demonstrate competence as thinking performers when they show the following:

- an understanding of organisational strategy and of the influences on strategy, both internal and external

- thinking that is not limited to their own organisational level

- the ability to produce plans that will effectively implement strategy at the operational level

- the ability to evaluate the implications of their recommendations for action, thus ensuring that those recommendations are feasible and suit the needs of that particular organisational context

- knowledge of current thinking, in terms of research and general organisational practice, to inform their views.

Example

The following question is taken from Section A of the May 2004 PM&D examination paper:

> Critically review learning and development strategies in your organisation in terms of the impact that they have on organisational performance and staff motivation. Indicate ways in which these strategies can be improved. In your response, take account of research in this area.

This is an example of a question that requires students to demonstrate competence as *thinking performers*. It requires thinking that is strategic and not limited to their own organisational level, the ability to consider plans that will effectively implement learning and development strategies, and the ability to evaluate their recommendations. There is also the need to take into account relevant research.

The second concept is that CIPD professionals should be able to fulfil the role of 'business partner'; they must be capable of adding value to their employing organisations. CIPD candidates can indicate their competence to act as *business partners* when they show awareness of the need to:

- ensure understanding of key personnel and development (P&D) issues facing the organisation, at all levels

- work in collaboration with internal stakeholders in order to achieve P&D goals

- actively network to increase knowledge of the general business environment, and to inform and support their own professional activity

- be fully informed about the P&D implications of internal and external changes affecting the organisation

- keep up to date with developments in P&D; gather data and share knowledge, identifying ways in which P&D initiatives can add value to the business.

Example

The following question is taken from Section B of the November 2003 PM&D examination paper:

Specify and analyse up to *three* external environmental changes (these can be political, legal or economic) that have affected your organisation in recent years.

This is an example of a question that illustrates the requirement for students, in the business partner role, to be aware of the implications for their organisations of changes in the external environment.

Another example is provided in the May 2004 paper, Section B, whose relevance to the concept of the 'business partner' is self-explanatory:

On what grounds would you argue that the people management and development functions should take on the role as a 'business partner' in organisations?

In addition to the two key concepts of thinking performer and business partner, the aim of the standards is to produce CIPD members who are able to display a mix of the following 10 competencies:

- personal drive and effectiveness
- people management and leadership
- business understanding
- professional and ethical behaviour
- added-value result achievement
- continuing learning
- analytical and intuitive/creative thinking
- 'customer' focus
- strategic thinking
- communication, persuasion and interpersonal skills.

Students studying PM&D need to relate the business partner and thinking performer concepts to their studies and assessments, and be aware of the requirements in terms of the development of competencies. Thus in the examination, for example, do answers display an understanding of the needs of that particular business where relevant? Do candidates' recommendations 'add value'? Can they display a questioning attitude and analytical thinking? Are they capable of taking a 'helicopter view' and rising above the day-to-day detail to show strategic awareness? Can they transmit their ideas on paper in a logical and coherent form that is persuasive and is directed towards the target audience?

The requirements of the standards are not therefore to be seen as dry concepts or merely lists of words and phrases – they need to be interpreted and applied to the organisational realities that student practitioners face in their own employment, and to other settings. Similarly, the requirement for students to display analytical and creative thinking should be applied to the standards themselves, and to the concepts that underpin them: how are they relevant and applicable?

The two main concepts of the 'thinking performer' and 'business partner', and the 10 associated competencies can be seen as the required outcomes from the standards, that is, what practitioners should be able to demonstrate as CIPD professionals. Although they are specifically relevant to practitioners, they should also inform students' deliberations. In addition to these, there is the BACKUP framework, five competencies that are linked specifically to the PDS assessment system. The five competencies are as follows:

- **b**usiness focus
- **a**pplication **c**apability
- **k**nowledge of subject
- **u**nderstanding
- **p**ersuasion and presentation skills.

These are five competencies that students should specifically be able to demonstrate during the course of their studies and in their assessment. They are briefly reviewed below.

Business focus

This is the ability to make value-added contributions to corporate purposes. Students need to show an understanding of the needs of the business in recommendations that they make. Business focus also means that existing ways of doing things need to be evaluated against the criteria that they should add value.

To assist students in developing this competency, it is a good idea if they share information and work collaboratively with other students, as well as collecting information and asking questions within their own organisations. This helps to widen knowledge and understanding of the extent to which different organisations demonstrate such a business focus among the people who work for them, both generally and in HR. It is also a good idea to search the literature and Internet for examples of organisations that have world-class reputations for delivering top performance through people. Such cases can usefully be used to illustrate exam answers.

Application capability

This refers to the ability to develop and present practical cost-effective solutions to problems that are relevant to the particular circumstances faced by an organisation. It is tested particularly in Section A of the PM&D paper, but can also be relevant to certain of the questions in Section B.

In the examination, any recommendations need to show a direct link to the problem or issue under consideration, be sufficiently detailed to convince the examiner of the student's knowledge and understanding of the area in question, and be clearly justified and show awareness of costs and benefits.

One way for students to develop this competency is to address past Section A questions in study groups, and then for each group to present their recommendations to the rest of the cohort – for feedback and constructive criticism!

Knowledge of subject

Knowledge of the subject matter forms a basis for the other competencies and is vital to successful performance in the examination. Students should make sure that the material in the whole standard is understood, at least to the extent of being able to provide short paragraph-length answers to the questions in Section B of the PM&D exam. For Section A, in addition to the in-depth knowledge they need to answer their chosen question, students must also be able to demonstrate a holistic appreciation of HRM and its contribution to organisational performance. Students are therefore advised to have a broad familiarity with the indicative content in general, and a more in-depth familiarity with approximately 50 per cent of it.

In terms of reading, *People management and development* by Marchington and Wilkinson (2002) forms a suitable core text. This can be supplemented by making reference to other general HR/personnel texts, of which there are a wide variety, including those by Armstrong (2001), Torrington *et al* (2001), and Bratton and Gold (2003). The CIPD texts that support each of the generalist electives (resourcing, learning and development, relations, and reward) also provide useful material. Students also need to keep up to date with developments in PM&D, by reference to the *People Management* publication, or its online equivalent. The CIPD website also provides an invaluable source of information, and a summary of relevant research reports.

Understanding

Although an adequate level of knowledge of the subject matter is an essential prerequisite for successful exam performance, it is not in itself sufficient. Students also need to demonstrate a critical understanding of what they have learned. For most questions, students are required to move beyond the descriptive to provide explanation, analysis and evaluation. It is therefore important for students to adopt a questioning attitude to their reading, to their own organisation's approach to HR, and to examination questions.

Persuasion and presentation skills

Examiners appreciate that for the PM&D Section B questions, candidates have little time in which to produce perfectly structured answers if they are to produce seven answers within an hour. However they should aim at a minimum to write clearly and concisely. Within Section A, where one question is chosen from four, it is more important to structure the answer clearly. It is also vital that the answer is produced in the format requested (report, briefing notes, and so on).

In general, students need to: address the question posed; choose from alternatives to formulate a realistic answer; justify and cost recommendations; and write in a clear and well-structured manner that succeeds in convincing the reader. Where appropriate, they should also provide examples to support a particular answer and argument. These may be drawn from their own organisation, or one that they are familiar with. Such examples can be drawn from previous jobs, other students, or from the literature and professional journals.

The CIPD's People Management and Development Generalist Standard: an overview

The professional standards are structured around four fields, of which People Management and Development is one:

- core management
- people management and development

- management reporting/continuing professional development (CPD) (to which the concept of the thinking performer is central)

- generalist and specialist electives.

People Management and Development (PM&D) is a compulsory core for all candidates. It forms the spine for the entire Professional Development Scheme (PDS) and CIPD Standards.

The new Professional Standards set out the knowledge and competence that it is considered are required of a professional personnel/HR practitioner today. Some of the areas set out in the standards are subject to choice by the individual: choice of which route to take, and which electives are the most appropriate. PM&D, however, is compulsory. The main rationale for this is that there is a body of knowledge, understanding and competence that all CIPD professionals should have covered and be able to demonstrate, regardless of the type of organisation they work for, or of their current position or role. This applies whether they work in the public or private sector, for a unionised or non-unionised firm, specialise in one particular area, such as recruitment or training and development, or work in a generalist role.

PM&D thus covers all the key elements of personnel and development in the main generic areas of resourcing, development, relations, and reward.

There are a number of other key concepts and ideas that underpin the PM&D Standard. These are as follows:

- The concept of integration. Practitioners need to understand how their work is integrated with that of other HR specialists, line managers, consultants and other stakeholders. *Vertical integration* refers to the links between people management and the business strategy. *Horizontal integration* refers to the 'fit' between different personnel/HR policies and practices.

Example

An example question from Section B of the November 2003 PM&D paper that illustrates this requirement:

> Identify some barriers likely to prevent vertical integration of human resources (HR) and business strategy being implemented within organisations. Discuss the extent to which these barriers apply in your organisation.

- In addition, it is necessary to consider not only how the different components of HRM at work interrelate with each other, but also the applicability of these in a wide range of different organisational contexts. In simple terms, HRM policies and practices that work well in one setting may not be directly applicable in a different organisational context. Rather than proposing 'best practice' solutions, consideration needs to be given to developing and implementing 'good practice' solutions that are contingent on the particular situation and set of circumstances, and having the ability to demonstrate clearly why this is the case.

- Practitioners need to gain the commitment of other stakeholders, such as line managers or the board of directors, to their recommendations and advice. Clearly demonstrating how these recommendations, advice and solutions can add value for the organisation is key to this.

Example

An example question taken from Section A of the Specimen PM&D paper that illustrates the above requirement:

> Your chief executive has asked you to prepare an outline paper indicating how people management and development strategy in an organisation of your choice might be integrated with organisation strategy and thereby contribute to improved organisational performance. Draft this paper, providing any necessary background information about this organisation to justify your response.

- Change and change management are an important aspect of the PM&D Standard. Practitioners need awareness of the changing nature of work and employment and the changing responsibilities for the management of HRM, as set out in Chapters 2 and 5 respectively of Marchington and Wilkinson (2002). They also need to be able to demonstrate change management skills, which form part of Chapter 5.

- PM&D provides a springboard for further learning and development. It both provides a basis for the generalist and specialist electives, and for ongoing CPD.

The above points have important implications for PM&D students. They need to be able to encompass the broad range of subject matter covered and comprehend the linkages and crossovers. Thus while resourcing, development, relations and reward may be studied separately as subject areas within PM&D, their interrelatedness needs to be appreciated. This is partly because many topics straddle two or more subject boundaries. Thus performance management, for example, has resourcing, development and reward issues at the very least; equal opportunities and diversity likewise; and information technology has relevance to many different aspects of PM&D. In addition, from a practitioner's perspective, real-life day-to-day HR problems tend not to come in neatly defined packages. They are more likely to be a messy amalgam of different, and possibly competing or even contradictory, issues.

Second, as well as combining and integrating the, at times, disparate elements of a broad subject, PM&D students also need to demonstrate strategic awareness. This is by no means easy, particularly when one's role is at an operational level seemingly distant or distinct from the strategic pinnacle. It is not made easier by the fact that many organisations appear either not to have a clear strategy, or have an espoused strategy that is either poorly communicated or badly implemented.

Third, students need to be able to tailor their recommendations to suit particular circumstances. For example, HR policies and practices that will suit a multinational are unlikely to be equally applicable to a small regional firm.

Fourth, in the examination, students need to propose solutions that, as well as being relevant, are persuasive, show an appreciation of the cost implications, and are clearly communicated in a relevant format and directed at the target audience. These issues are explored more fully in Chapter 3 on exam preparation.

Fifth, as well as demonstrating an awareness of change and change management skills, students need to keep up to date with developments in the field and with legislative changes. *People Management*, for example, has a regular update of research news and of new legislation. The CIPD also produces a range of research summaries, fact sheets, surveys and reports, which students need to familiarise themselves with. Much of this information is available on the CIPD website.

Content of the People Management and Development Standard

PM&D forms one of the four fields of the Professional Standards. The standards in total set out the requirements for a CIPD professional. Each field sets out the particular standards for that field.

The PM&D Standard, like the other CIPD Standards, breaks down into three parts:

Purpose

This gives the rationale for PM&D as a compulsory core for all candidates and as a spine for the other standards.

Performance indicators

These provide a way of understanding the standard of performance required by those entering the field. There are 14 performance indicators for PM&D, which are provided under two headings: operational indicators and knowledge performance indicators.

Operational indicators define what practitioners must be able to do. The 14 operational indicators for PM&D are thus all examples of how students should be able to demonstrate their learning at work as a result of studying this core subject. By definition they cannot be examined in a conventional written form, except as a record of achievement, feeding into a CPD log perhaps. The opportunity to practise and demonstrate competence in these operational indicators will often present themselves on a day-to-day basis in the course of your role at work; at other times you will need to seek them out. Opportunities may also arise as part of the skills element of the course you are studying. Marchington and Wilkinson's (2002) core PM&D textbook also includes activities that relate to these indicators, examples of which are given below.

Practitioners must be able to:

1. Implement appropriate PM&D policies that maximise the contribution of people to organisational objectives and wider societal needs.

2. Supply accurate and timely advice on the rights and obligations of employers and employees arising from the contract of employment and associated legislation, bearing in mind conflicts of interest and issues of confidentiality.

Example
Page 72 in Chapter 3 of Marchington and Wilkinson (2002) outlines a relevant activity.

---

3. Access, use and interpret data from a range of internal and published sources in preparing and presenting reports.

4. Contribute effectively to the planning, design and implementation of projects.

Example
Chapter 5 of Marchington and Wilkinson (2002) provides some relevant activities.

---

5. Manipulate people management and development databases, and provide advice on how to interpret the information and results they produce.

6. Demonstrate an ethical approach to PM&D.

> **Example**
> The section on ethics in Chapter 6 of Marchington and Wilkinson (2002) lists two relevant activities.

7. Contribute to the effective implementation of appropriate PM&D policies in different types of organisations.

8. Work in partnership with other stakeholders to help overcome blockages and barriers to change.

9. Make recommendations about the advantages and disadvantages of outsourcing some or all elements of PM&D.

> **Example**
> Chapter 9 of Marchington and Wilkinson (2002) provides some relevant activities.

10. Provide and use benchmarks and other measures to assess the contribution of PM&D to organisational success.

11. Implement and operate cost-effective processes for recruiting and retaining the right calibre of staff for their organisation.

12. Contribute to the design, development and delivery of learning and training and to utilise measures to evaluate their effectiveness in supporting organisational goals.

> **Example**
> Chapters 12 and 13 of Marchington and Wilkinson (2002) provide some relevant activities.

13. Work in partnership with other stakeholders to develop procedures and processes that enhance the commitment of employees and resolve conflict at work.

14. Provide advice about how to motivate and reward people so as to maximise employee contributions to organisational performance.

Knowledge indicators define what practitioners must understand and be able to explain. These are thus easier to assess in written examinations than the operational indicators outlined above.

The PM&D Standard's 14 performance knowledge indicators are as follows. Practitioners must understand and be able to explain:

1. The implications for the effective management and development of people that arise from the changing nature of work and employment.

2. The context within which PM&D takes place in terms of government actions, legal requirements and wider societal needs.

3. The relationship between employing organisations and the economic and institutional frameworks within which they operate.

4. The role of research and change management skills in organisations.

5. The role of information technology in supporting PM&D.

6. The nature and importance of ethics, professionalism, equal opportunities and managing diversity.

7. The meaning of strategic management and its implications for PM&D.

8. How different aspects of personnel and development are integrated with each other, with business strategy and with organisational structures and cultures.

9. The ways in which PM&D is implemented by line managers, functional specialists and consultants, and how these interact with each other.

10. The contribution that PM&D can make to organisational success.

11. How effective recruitment, selection and performance management can contribute to organisational effectiveness.

12. How effective learning and training processes can contribute to enhanced employee skills and organisational performance.

13. How effective employment relations can contribute to increased employee potential and commitment.

14. How effective reward management practices can contribute to enhanced employee motivation and satisfaction at work.

Indicative content

This provides more detail, and indicates the level and context. It is on this detailed content that the examination questions are likely to be based, so candidates need to familiarise themselves with this over the course of their studies.

Once again, it should be stressed that the indicators are not meant to be viewed as discrete areas; they will need to be combined and integrated. Examination questions may well cover more than one indicator.

The following section of this chapter contains an outline of the indicators, together with a summary of the requirements and implications of each. It also groups them together into appropriate sub-groupings. The relevant chapters of Marchington and Wilkinson (2002) are mapped against the standards.

Shaping the PM&D agenda (Part 2 of Marchington and Wilkinson)

The first three knowledge indicators can be grouped together under the heading 'Shaping the PM&D agenda'. They examine how the PM&D agenda is shaped by a number of issues and institutions, as well as broader political, economic, social and technological trends. While such issues and trends are very influential, it is important not to view them in a totally deterministic manner. As Marchington and Wilkinson (2002, p18) point out, in the last 20 years changes in the macro-economic environment – especially changes in patterns of employment and in legislation – have clearly affected the nature of the employment relationship as well as the practice of HR. Nevertheless, although such wider developments do have a significant impact, their precise influence is heavily dependent on the specific circumstances in which a particular organisation operates.

The above highlights two of the major themes that were introduced in the earlier sections of this chapter, which those studying

PM&D need to be aware of and to apply, as both students and as practitioners:

- First, although organisations may be subject to the same or similar broad external influences, the specific outcome of these influences will vary according to the particular situation of any specific organisation and how it chooses to react. Thus some firms flourish in a recession while others fail; some choose a cost-cutting strategy while others choose to invest. Furthermore, the broad general influences (economic trends, legislation) will combine with the particular circumstances of specific organisations to create a unique scenario.

- Second, HR practitioners need to understand both the implications of these broad and specific influences for HR and the management of people, and how the choice of HR action can itself have a strong influencing factor. Thus a decision may be made to invest in training and development despite recessionary pressures. In short, there is a need to be both responsive and proactive.

Also central to this section of the standards is the notion of the employment relationship, whether in terms of the direct employment of staff by an organisation, or in the subcontracting of work to external bodies or use of agency staff. Both parties to the relationship (employer and employee or worker) are likely to share commonalties of interest (in the success of the enterprise, for example), but they are also likely to have differences of interest (regarding the effort–reward bargain, for example). Thus the relationship is likely to be characterised by both co-operation and conflict, and at times by confusion and contradiction. The balance of power between the two parties is also likely to vary in different circumstances.

1. The implications for people management of the changing context of work

Practitioners who are effective in the first indicator are able to implement appropriate PM&D policies that maximise the contribution of people to organisational objectives and reflect wider societal needs. Through coverage of the topics outlined in the indicative content, they are able to demonstrate an appreciation of the following:

- the changing nature of work

- the flexibility debate, new organisational forms such as outsourcing and public–private partnerships, and the ways in which these are reshaping work and employment relations

- the changing nature of the employment relationship and attitudes towards work, including questions about job satisfaction, motivation and organisational commitment, the psychological contract and work intensification.

Example

From Section B of the November 2003 PM&D paper:

What do research studies suggest that employees want from their working lives? Evaluate how your organisation satisfies (or does not satisfy) these needs for its employees.

These three themes that form the first indicator recur in other parts of the PM&D Standards.

For this indicator students/practitioners need an appreciation of current labour market and employment trends, with particular reference to the proportion of workers on 'atypical contracts', such as temporary and part-time. Publications such as *Labour Market Trends* form a useful source for such data, and they are also summarised, with supporting commentary, in newspaper and HR journal articles. *The Workplace Industrial/Employee Relations* series also provides useful analyses. An appreciation of the possible implications for HR of these trends is also needed. This area overlaps with Indicator 3.

An understanding of the flexible firm model (Atkinson 1984, and Atkinson and Meager 1986) is also required, together with an evaluation of the applicability of such models in practice. Students should be able to debate the relative advantages and disadvantages of different types of flexible working, for both employer and worker.

Lastly, students need an appreciation of the employment relationship, and of different perspectives on this relationship. Related to this are people's expectations of work and the psychological contract. What do people want from work? How do UK workers feel that employers are treating them? Students should be able to make reference to studies on the state of the psychological contract, such as those by Guest and Conway for the CIPD. Students should also be able to debate such questions as the extent to which employment is becoming more insecure, and whether work is becoming more intensive and people are working longer hours.

The above clearly demonstrates the need for students to have an appreciation of current issues and knowledge of relevant data and studies. In other words, they need to keep up to date. This section also requires students to be able to question and debate current issues rather than just repeat a particular viewpoint, and to consider the implications of various issues and trends for particular organisations, including their own. It thus forms a good illustration of the requirement to be thinking performers.

2. The context within which PM&D takes place in terms of government actions, legal requirements and wider societal needs

The first indicator involves an analysis of the way in which the work and employment context provides a backcloth for the practice of HRM. The approach to such an analysis needs to be multi-layered, since the precise nature of the employment relationship in a particular organisational situation will be the result of a combination of both internal decisions and external influences, with the latter being the result of an interplay between local, national and international forces.

The second indicator focuses on the legal framework, and associated institutions. Practitioners must be able to provide accurate and timely advice on the rights and obligations of employers and employees arising from the contract of employment and associated legislation. The indicative content encompasses the following:

- the role of the law in shaping HRM at work, including a consideration of European developments

- individual and collective rights at work

- the role of employment tribunals (ETs) and the commissions, particularly those relating to equal opportunities, racial equality, health and safety, and trade union issues.

Once again, the material that forms this particular indicator also informs others, since the law has an impact on many different areas of HR.

As stated above, practitioners need to have an up-to-date knowledge of employment law, and the ability to apply this knowledge in the provision of relevant advice. Law textbooks such as Lewis and Sargeant (2002) provide more in-depth coverage, and *People Management* and its online equivalent provide timetables of legislative changes, while publications such as the *Industrial Relations Law Report* and *IRS Employment Trends* provide more detailed coverage and cases. The aim of this indictor is not, however, to produce legal experts, and practitioners need to be aware of the limits in their own expertise and know when to consult relevant specialists.

Students need to appreciate the direct and indirect impact of bodies such as employment tribunals, directly in terms of cases brought before the tribunal, but also the indirect influence in the message these send to employers about how to deal with disciplinary and other issues. Students also need to show an awareness of the debates surrounding the increased coverage of employment law, such as the 'flexibility versus individual protection' debate.

3. Economic and institutional frameworks for PM&D

The third indicator requires knowledge of labour market statistics and trends, such as employment and unemployment rates, both in aggregate and with reference to gender and age, and the shift from manufacturing to services employment. It thus overlaps with the first indicator and shares with it the same requirement for up-to-date statistics and information, and the same sources of such information. It also requires an appreciation of the institutional forces that influence PM&D in the workplace. Practitioners must be able to access, use and interpret data from a range of sources. The indicative content falls into the following categories:

- labour market and employment data; national, sectoral and local patterns of labour supply

- initiatives in training, learning and skills development

- the principal institutions that influence people management and development in the workplace.

The requirement for an appreciation of labour market and employment statistics and trends has already been reviewed above. The second area examines the changing nature of the training system, from its earlier roots in industrial training boards through to Sector Skills Councils (SSCs) and the Learning and Skills Councils (LSCs) as well as a consideration of vocational qualifications (NVQs). The main institutions for consideration are trade unions and the Trades Union Congress (TUC), employers' associations and the Confederation of British Industry (CBI), and the Advisory, Conciliation and Arbitration Service (ACAS) and Central Arbitration Committee (CAC).

Some relevant questions for students to debate include the current and future role of trade unions; the relevance of social partnerships; and the role of ACAS in promoting good practice. Students need to be aware of recent legal changes that have affected the role of ACAS and the CAC.

Example
From Section B of the May 2004 PM&D paper:

> Making sure that you take into account research evidence in the field, examine why trade union membership has declined during the past two decades.

The PM&D contribution (Part 3 of Marchington and Wilkinson)

The next three performance indicators can be grouped under the heading 'The PM&D contribution'. They examine how HR practitioners can make a distinctive contribution to performance.

4. The role of research and change management skills in organisations

5. The role of information technology in supporting PM&D

These two indicators are, each in their own way, somewhat different from the others. Indicator 4 is skills-based. HR practitioners are often involved in project work with other managers and achieving outcomes through the actions of other people. Relevant skills include planning and design, communication, interviewing, managing time, accessing, analysing and presenting data using statistical sources and information technology (which encompasses Indicator 5) and persuasion skills. The main vehicle for covering and assessing these skills in the standards is via the 'research project'.

Example
From Section A of the November 2003 PM&D paper:

> Your manager has come to accept that carrying out research projects is a critical part of the people management and development function because it is an effective tool for influencing line managers. However, she has never received any formal research training. As you are on a Chartered Institute of Personnel and Development (CIPD) course, she has asked you to brief her on the range of methods used in collecting research data and the circumstances in which they are best employed. Prepare a paper responding to this request, making sure that you provide people management and development examples to illustrate your response.

In addition, HR practitioners need to be able to implement recommendations for change and overcome resistance to change. Marchington and Wilkinson (2002, pp137–140) set out Buchanan and Boddy's five competence clusters required for people to be effective change agents, and Mayan-White's key features and methods of a change management strategy.

Indicator 5 relates to the above in that IT provides methods for accessing, analysing and presenting data. Information technology is also integrated throughout the PM&D Standards, as IT provides a support tool for PM&D.

6. The nature and importance of ethics, professionalism, equal opportunities and managing diversity

Practitioners need to demonstrate an ethical approach to PM&D. Commitment to certain agreed standards is central to this. The indicator examines the growth and development of a specialist personnel and development function and the need to adopt a professional and ethical stance on HR issues. On occasions the HR function has been regarded as the conscience of employers, there to ensure that, in the pursuit of more efficient and productive work, the human dimension is not overlooked. Compliance with legal obligations and mainte- nance of mechanisms for employee voice are two aspects of this, yet professionalism should also relate to how organisations can achieve greater success through the adoption of up-to-date and proven HR good practice. The challenge for HR practitioners is often to persuade line managers of the case for this. Equal opportunities and diversity is just one area where professionalism and ethics combine, and where a business case can be made in addition to the moral one.

Example
From Section B of the November 2003 paper:

> Examine the ethical principles that should underpin the activities of people management and development profes- sionals. Discuss one example in an organisation known to you, where its business practices conflict with these ethical principles.

The indicative content centres on the following:

- the growth and development of a specialist P&D function

- professionalism, the role of the CIPD and CPD

- business ethics and social responsibility

- discrimination and disadvantage at work; equality management and managing diversity.

Students should be aware of the possible tensions that may arise for HR in striving for business goals at the same time as maintaining professionalism. However, a strong professional and ethical stance can also provide HR practitioners with a potentially distinctive contribution to improved performance.

Students should also be aware of trends in the provision of

family-friendly policies by firms, and be aware of recent, current and proposed legislative developments in this and related areas.

Integrating the PM&D contribution (Part 4 of Marchington and Wilkinson)

The next four indicators are based around the concept of integration – the integration of the PM&D contribution in order to deliver higher levels of organisational performance.

7. Strategic management and its implications for HRM

The need for students to be able to show strategic awareness has already been highlighted as one of the key requirements of the PM&D Standards. This can prove to be a challenge when working at an operational level. To overcome this difficulty, students need to gain an appreciation of the strategy process and of the different theoretical approaches to strategy, as well as an understanding of why organisational reality may be very different. Such an insight should engender the ability to produce practical recommendations on how to begin to implement strategic plans at their own organisational level. This is the key: PM&D practitioners need to be able to contribute to the effective implementation of policies that are appropriate for that particular business, and that contribute to the achievement of corporate goals.

In summary, what HR does needs to help the organisation achieve its ultimate goals, and HR needs to be able to demonstrate this.

Example

From Section A of the May 2004 PM&D paper:

Your chief executive officer (CEO) has heard about the research literature on the 'resource-based' view (RBV) of the firm but does not fully understand what it means. He has asked you to draft a briefing paper explaining the meaning of the term and its relationship to sustained competitive advantage. He is particularly interested in how the RBV of the firm can be linked to people management and development issues within an organisation. Write your paper making sure that you cover all these issues.

The indicative content covers the following areas:

- corporate and business strategy; different models and approaches

- human resource management as a driver, as strategic partner and as an agent of implementation

- the resource-based view of the firm and implications for PM&D.

This indicator requires an understanding of different approaches to corporate and business strategy. Students also need to demonstrate an understanding of the possible roles for HR: in leading strategy formulation itself, in acting as a strategic partner, or in simply acting as an agent of implementation.

8. The integration of different aspects of personnel and development

The indicative content of this indicator covers the following:

- the link between organisation strategy and HR strategy; vertical integration and 'best fit'

- converting organisational and HR strategy into practice; blockages and barriers to implementation and overcoming these

- horizontal integration and 'best practice'; integration of different elements of PM&D.

This standard is closely linked to the previous one. It further develops the possible links between the strategy of the organisation on the one hand, and HR policies and practice on the other. Such linkages are referred to as 'vertical integration'. This encompasses the notion of 'best fit', or contingency. As such it provides a theoretical explanation as to why, in practice, HRM in say a leading pharmaceutical firm might differ from that in a small textile factory. It thus provides a useful contrast to ideas of best practice. These ideas are further developed in the following indicator. The difficulties involved in these linkages, and in converting strategy into practice, are also explored.

Example
From Section B of the May 2004 PM&D paper:

> Identify some major barriers likely to prevent vertical integration of human resources (HR) and business strategy being implemented within organisations. Discuss the extent to which these barriers apply in your organisation.

As a corollary to the concept of vertical integration, the indicator also encompasses ideas of horizontal integration. In relation to PM&D, this refers to the extent to which different HR policies link to, and are consistent with, each other. This is of particular significance to the PM&D Standard. PM&D covers the main generic areas of personnel/HR: resourcing, development, relations and reward. The argument propounded in this indicator is that, in any one organisation, the policies and practices in these areas need to be consistent: that is, that the total is more than the simple sum of the parts. An example of lack of 'fit' would be an individual performance pay approach to reward, at the same time as trying to engender teamwork.

The notion of horizontal integration leads on to that of 'bundles' of human resource practices, that is, a set of practices that in isolation mean little, but in coherent combination become powerful drivers of organisational performance. From here it is but a short step to proposing 'bundles' of best practice. Best-practice or high-commitment models of HRM propose that it is possible to identify a set of human resource practices that consistently deliver higher levels of organisational performance. These ideas are revisited in Indicator 10.

9. The implementation of HRM: changing responsibilities

HR specialists can take on a variety of different possible roles. Students need to be familiar with the different models of the HR function (Legge, Tyson and Fell, Storey and so on) and their application. Within the broad context of 'people management' there is also the associated question as to what should be the preserve of HR specialists, and what line managers should undertake. Several surveys (such as Hutchinson and Wood, 1995) have pointed to line managers gaining increased responsibility for HR issues, particularly in relation to practical implementation rather than policy formulation. PM&D practitioners need the ability to work with line managers, both in a supportive role and more proactively in suggesting initiatives.

Other trends have seen a number of organisations increase their use of HR consultants, and the delivery of HR through shared services and in some cases call centres. Outsourcing HR either partially or completely is another possibility.

Example
From Section A of the May 2004 PM&D paper:

You have been asked to write an article for the business supplement of the local newspaper which is running a series looking at contemporary management practices in firms in your geographical area. The title of this proposed article is: 'Outsourcing people management and development activities: when to do it and why'. Draft this article bearing in mind your target audiences and their likely knowledge about people management and development activities. Justify your response.

The example above raises a number of important issues and questions relating to how HR can and will be delivered, and to the future of the HR function as traditionally viewed.

The indicative content of the indicator covers the following:

- line managers and PM&D, implications of devolution of HR activities

- consultants and PM&D

- different ways of organising and delivering the HR function, including outsourcing.

10. The contribution of PM&D to organisational success

The previous indicator raised questions about the organisation and delivery of HR in organisations. Such questions, in parallel with business pressures, have led to the need for HR departments to justify their existence and demonstrate how they 'add value'.

One way of increasing the likelihood that organisations take HR issues seriously, and thus arguably enhance the contribution of the function, is to have a specialist personnel presence on the board. In terms of assessing the effectiveness of HR, one method is to ask key stakeholders in the organisation for their views. Such 'customers' may include line managers, chief executives and employees. It is difficult for HR professionals to measure the effectiveness of their own function directly, particularly given that their contribution to organisational goals is mediated through line managers. Two possibilities, however, are first to carry out benchmarking exercises, and second to focus on internal evaluations – by drawing up service-level agreements, for example, or using a range of quantitative and qualitative data.

Lastly, the link between HRM – and in particular, best-practice high-commitment HRM – and performance has now become a major research area. In the United Kingdom this includes work by David Guest and his colleagues for the CIPD. Although questions remain concerning the research itself and the specific mix of HR practices required, there is now growing evidence for a strong correlation between people management and business performance.

Example

From Section B of the November 2003 PM&D paper:

> Examine why it is difficult to measure the contribution of the people management and development function to improved organisational performance.

The indicative content for this indicator covers the following:

- evaluating the HR function, techniques and difficulties

- gaining support for P&D interventions
- the contribution of HR practices to business performance.

PM&D in Practice (Part 5 of Marchington and Wilkinson)

The last four indicators are concerned with PM&D in practice, and cover people resourcing, learning and development, employee relations, and employee reward. These should be studied and applied in the context of the previous 10 indicators. Thus, to what extent is a proposed practical intervention likely to add value? How does it integrate with other HR practices, and with the HR and overall strategy of the organisation? How can it best be delivered and evaluated? The four indicators are briefly reviewed below.

11. Effective recruitment, selection and performance management

This indicator focuses on cost-effective recruitment and selection, and managing performance for added value. The indicative content covers the following:

- human resource planning
- recruitment and selection methods and their application
- induction and employee socialisation
- performance management and appraisal
- managing poor performance, and attendance management.

As a result of this indicator, practitioners need to be able to implement cost-effective processes for recruiting and retaining the right calibre of staff.

Example
From Section B of the November 2003 PM&D paper:

Analyse how an effective attendance management policy adds value (or could add value) to your organisation.

---

12. Effective learning and training

This indicator focuses on how effective learning and training can contribute to enhanced employee skills and organisational performance. The indicative content covers the following:

- individual learning; learning styles
- organisational learning and the concept of the learning organisation
- the training cycle and its application
- evaluating the effectiveness of training events and learning processes.

As a result of the indicator, practitioners should be able to contribute to the design, development and delivery of learning and training, and to utilise measures to evaluate their effectiveness in supporting organisational goals.

Example
From Section B of the May 2004 PM&D paper:

What are the main features of modern apprenticeships? Review some of the problems in implementing such apprenticeships.

---

13. Effective employee relations

This indicator examines how effective employee relations can contribute to increased employee potential and commitment. The indicative content covers the following:

- structures and processes for effective employee relations
- differing approaches to the management of employee relations
- resolving differences: grievance and disciplinary handling, bargaining
- gaining employee commitment: communication and employee voice.

As a result of this indicator, practitioners should be able to work in partnership with other stakeholders to develop procedures and processes that enhance the commitment of employees and resolve conflict at work.

Example
From Section B of the May 2004 PM&D paper:

> Explain the principles underpinning the term 'partnership agreement' between an employer and a trade union. What evidence is there to show that both partners gain from such agreements?

---

14. Effective reward management

This indicator covers how effective reward management practices can contribute to enhanced employee motivation and satisfaction at work. The indicative content covers the following:

- the role of reward in the motivation of staff
- different methods of pay and reward
- equity and fairness in reward
- harmonisation and non-financial rewards and benefits.

As a result of this indicator, practitioners should be able to provide advice about how to motivate and reward people so as to maximise employee contributions to organisational performance.

Example

From Section A of the May 2004 PM&D paper:

> The local college of further and higher education has asked you to give a short presentation to a small group of business studies students on the advantages and disadvantages of performance related pay (PRP) in organisations. Using research findings on PRP, outline what you would say in the presentation. Justify your response.

The last four indicators and their supporting indicative content have been briefly outlined above. It should be noted, however, that they should not be seen in isolation but integrated both with each other, and with the preceding 10. The discussions that informed the other indicators should also be applied to these. There is also the requirement to keep up to date with developments in the four areas of resourcing, learning and development, relations and reward.

Conclusion

The aim of this chapter has been to provide an overview of the PM&D Standard and the field to which it relates. Detail has been provided of the relevant performance indicators and indicative content that students will need to be familiar with when preparing for their examinations.

The next chapter provides some general advice on how to revise and how to tackle the examination itself.

SECTION 2

HOW TO TACKLE REVISION AND THE EXAMINATION

2 REVISION AND EXAMINATION GUIDANCE

Introduction

The purpose of this chapter is to give outline advice on how to prepare and revise for the People Management and Development (PM&D) examination. Further information can be found by making reference to the CIPD's guides to effective study (Guide 3) and to examinations (Guide 6) which are available on its website. Another useful source of information is Ellie Chambers and Andrew Northedge's book *The arts good study guide* (1997).

Preparing for the examination

Like an athlete preparing for the Olympic Games, the examination should be viewed as the culmination of an ongoing process that starts with the commencement of the course of study. Where relevant, regular attendance at, and contribution to, classes, good note-taking, reading and updating of subject knowledge will all help to ensure success.

Time management

Time management is of importance from the beginning of your course, but becomes increasingly so as the examination draws near. As Chambers and Northedge (1997) point out, when students first start studying they can find it difficult at first simply because it has no 'shape'. What is needed is some sort of structure – an idea of what needs to be done and when, otherwise a lot of time can be wasted dithering about.

Managing time involves two interrelated elements: finding enough of it, and then using it effectively. One way of tackling the former is to draw up a chart of your typical week. You can then begin to work out the total study time you can reasonably expect to set aside and where in the week it falls. Even if you find that it is not always possible to stick exactly to the plan, it is still worth making the effort, because the decisions you make in changing your plans force you to think about what you are doing and why. Planning makes you think strategically instead of just drifting about.

Once you have found the time, the next challenge is to use it effectively. This involves having an appreciation of the demands of the task in question. You will find that for some tasks (such as reading a fairly difficult article or attempting some past examination questions), you need to be reasonably fresh and have a definable amount of time available, while others (such as organising your notes) you can fit into the odd moment and manage even when you are tired.

Another problem is if the tasks themselves are poorly defined. With a large over-riding task, like revising for the PM&D examination, it is important that this is broken down into a series of smaller sub-tasks. This is explored further below.

Revision

Revision is a necessary evil, but can be made easier with some previous preparation. A suitable core textbook, such as Marchington and Wilkinson (2002), should be purchased and referred to regularly throughout the programme.

Key passages can be highlighted and relevant sections drawn attention to by sticky-backed notes. Familiarity with a core text provides a useful basis for further reading in specific topic areas.

It is also useful to have a large ring binder with subdividers. This can be used to collect and classify relevant articles by topic, such as 'performance management', 'legal updates' or 'equal opportunities and diversity'. These topic areas can be cross-referenced with the relevant sections in the textbook and form a structured basis for revision. Integration of topics can be achieved by linking topics together, applying them to different scenarios, and practising past examination questions.

In terms of the topics themselves, for PM&D Chapter 1 of this revision guide lists the 14 key knowledge indicators and outlines the relevant indicative content. These form a useful starting point for identifying key topic areas and a useful basis for further subdivision.

We can take the ninth indicator as an example – 'the ways in which people management and development is implemented by line managers, functional specialists and consultants, and how these interact with each other'. One sub-section of this is the outsourcing of HR activities. This could then be further subdivided for revision purposes into the different categories of HR consultants, the arguments for outsourcing, the possible problems, and a list of relevant examples and studies.

It is advisable to start formal revision at least a month before the examination itself. Revision sessions can be based around particular topics. For each topic, relevant theories/models should be identified and their application evaluated. Key authors should be noted and their articles summarised. A similar approach should be taken to the application of research findings and organisational examples.

Thus, to take one topic as an example – the link between people management practices and organisational performance – students may well have appropriate lecture notes or class exercises, and should have read the relevant section of the core text. This could form the basis of revision notes. The CIPD website provides research summaries, and this particular area is well covered. Students should make note of the key points of, say, the findings of John Purcell's investigations, in addition to those of David Guest and others for the CIPD. Note could be made of relevant recent articles in *People Management* such as that of 15 May 2003 by Purcell and colleagues highlighting how the way in which people are managed has affected the performance of four different Tesco stores.

Armed with the above information, students should be in a strong position to tackle a question on this subject. They should be able to demonstrate knowledge and understanding, and hopefully a questioning attitude that leads to analysis and evaluation (assuming such an attitude has informed their initial study and revision). They should also be able to make reference to relevant organisational examples. As long as they address the question as set (rather than merely listing everything they know in this area), they should do well.

Such an approach to study, and subsequent revision, will generate a large amount of relevant material. It is important that this is well organised and classified. Reading through notes on a particular topic, the key information can then be highlighted. This can then form the basis of condensed revision notes under key subheadings. Students familiar with the mind-mapping techniques of Tony Buzan may find these helpful here; an alternative is to simply make lists or bullet points. This process can then be repeated until each topic is summarised and condensed down to its essential components.

General advice on the PM&D examination

Format of the examination

The examination is in two sections, A and B. The time allowed is two hours plus 10 minutes reading time. Each section is equally weighted, so approximately one hour should be spent on each.

In Section A, students have a choice of one from four questions. Each of the questions in this section requires students to carry out an assignment or task with reference to a particular area of HR. The question may require them to relate their answer to their own organisation, or may relate to some other scenario, such as the preparation for a talk to the local CIPD branch. They may be asked to present their answer in the form of a report, or some other format, such as the design of a training programme, an outline for a talk to be presented, or a letter to be written to a newspaper. It is essential that students comply with these instructions. Students who write essays here, for example, will not pass. It is also vital that an analytical and evaluative approach is taken that considers the question in relation to the wider business context and with reference to relevant literature on the subject, and that provides examples of practice in other organisations as appropriate.

In Section B, students must answer seven questions from 10. Again, about an hour should be allocated to this section. Each question is capable of being answered in seven or eight minutes through relatively short answers. The questions can be drawn from anywhere in the PM&D Standard. This section therefore requires students to present the essential information relating to the area of the question in order to demonstrate their knowledge and understanding. By necessity, answers must be concise, but they can be supplemented with illustrative examples and reference to reading that demonstrates students' wider understanding of the issue. As with the previous section, it is crucial that students analyse and evaluate the issue in question rather than merely providing uncritical description. It is also vitally important that all seven questions are tackled.

Analysis and evaluation

The importance of producing answers that are analytical and evaluative, rather than merely descriptive, is stressed above. But what is actually meant by these terms?

- To *analyse* means to critically examine the elements of something complex, using logic. It is arguing by force of reason. If you want to dispute a claim made by someone else, you are expected to use argument and evidence.
- To *evaluate* means to weigh up both sides and make a judgement.

As an example, take an analytical and evaluative approach to the possibility of a link between people management practices and organisational performance. What is the evidence that certain practices lead to improved performance? You need to critically examine the studies that argue for the link, then the question marks and queries, before drawing your own conclusions based not on gut feeling or preconceptions, but on the balance of the arguments.

Level

The Professional Development Scheme is a Master's-level (M-level) programme, which means that students must display:

- a systematic understanding of knowledge and a critical awareness of current problems and/or new insights

- a comprehensive understanding of techniques

- a conceptual understanding that enables both current research and methodologies to be evaluated critically

- originality in the application of knowledge

- the ability to deal with complex issues both systematically and creatively, make sound judgements in the absence of complete data and communicate conclusions

- the demonstration of self-direction and originality in tackling and solving problems

- a continued drive to advance knowledge, understanding and skills (principally through CPD).

Because the PDS is an M-level programme, it is also essential that students keep themselves informed about research and wider organisational practice. This can be achieved by regularly reading the research columns of *Shine* and *People Management*, visiting the CIPD's research website (www.cipd.co.uk/research), attending events such as those held by the local CIPD branch, and reading the core text and other texts that contain reference to research studies and examples of organisational practice.

The CIPD expects PM&D students to be aware of the key findings of its various research reports, summaries of which are available on the website, but does not expect students to have in-depth knowledge of them.

Exam technique

Students need to ensure that they allocate their time correctly in the examination. The 10 minutes reading time should be made full use of. One suggested technique is to quickly 'skim read' the whole paper, and then read through it again carefully, noting key requirements, words or phrases. Equal time (one hour) should be allocated to each section. For the short-answer questions in Section B, approximately seven to eight minutes should be allocated to each of the seven answers. Candidates should avoid the temptation to spend much more time on answering questions that they find easier or know a lot about. Any spare time at the end can be used to check through answers, making any corrections or additions.

Answers to questions should be reasonably structured so that points are made in a logical sequence and the answer 'flows'. This is particularly relevant to the answer to the chosen question in Section A, since it will be longer than the Section B answers. Students may find that sketching out a brief answer plan helps to order their thoughts and to structure their answer, but any such plan should be brief.

It is of vital importance in the examination that students answer the question. The importance of this cannot be stressed too much. Students may be tempted to write everything they know about a particular topic area, or to answer a question as they wish it had been set, but this will not gain them marks. Students must address the question as set. It may help here to underline or highlight the key words in the question.

Where candidates are asked to relate their answer to their own organisation, this can be interpreted loosely as meaning the one they currently work for or one with which they are familiar. This familiarity could have been gained through their own or others' experience, or by reading about the organisation in a textbook, periodical article or on the Internet. This obviously applies where a candidate is not currently employed, but is also relevant where a student's own organisation has few or no relevant examples to offer. In answering such questions it is important to give enough information about the organisation selected to enable the examiner to assess the relevance of the candidate's answer to that particular context. It is vital for candidates to show why their proposals or recommendations are suited to that particular organisation.

In terms of length of answer, while it is expected that candidates will be able to write reasonably extensively on their chosen questions, it is quality not quantity as such that counts. High-quality answers can also be concise. Lengthy answers can fail if they are poorly informed, or not adequately focused. Time is also a major constraint here – for Section B answers, how much can a candidate write that is relevant and focused on the question in seven to eight minutes? This is likely to be between three-quarters of a page and a page, but will vary with the style of writing.

Guidance to candidates from CIPD examiners

The section below summarises some of the basic things that students need to do in order to pass the written examination.

The essentials

. Read as widely as you can during your period of study. Do not just rely upon the core text but also draw upon relevant academic journals, professional journals and recognised websites. This will enable you to take account of different viewpoints, competing

perspectives and research findings. Keep abreast with curren
developments.

2. Make sure that you have a good working knowledge and under
    standing of the PM&D Professional Standards. Work throug
    them, read around them and continually review them.

3. When revising, practise 'model' answers, basing these question
    on previous diets of examinations. If you are studying at
    recognised centre, do this in collaboration with your peers o
    the course/programme. You will be surprised how much yo
    can learn together, in study groups.

4. Manage your time effectively. Work out times for studying (c
    revising) particular topics, cover all the topics in the standard
    and learn them 'actively'. This means making notes, 'workin
    things out' and 'working things through'. Do not just rea
    'passively': you will fall asleep! Find out your optimum times fo
    studying and for how long you can concentrate. Normally stud
    in sequential, short 'time bytes' rather than long, uninterrupte
    periods. You will work more effectively in this way.

5. In the examination room, read the questions thoroughly an
    make sure that you understand what the examiner is asking yo
    to respond to (see below). Be relevant, and answer the questio
    set, not the question that you would like to have been asked. Stic
    to a time schedule to ensure that you answer all the questions tha
    you are required to do.

6. In the examination room, provide justifications to your answer
    when asked to.

7. In the examination room, write persuasively, authoritatively an
    legibly.

8. In the examination room, do not 'waffle' around the questio
    set. Identify the issue being examined, respond to it and stick th
    point behind the question.

Some reasons for getting good marks in the written examinatio

1. Candidates able to demonstrate understanding of the question
    set, underpinning knowledge of the topic, and the ability t

analyse and evaluate the research evidence relating to their answers are likely to be awarded high marks.

2. Answers that are well structured, logically presented and carefully argued are likely to be awarded high marks, provided again that the answers are relevant and to the point.

3. Answers that demonstrate effective wider reading and evidence-based research or professional practice are likely to be awarded high marks.

4. Candidates able to demonstrate critical analysis and systematic review of the examination topics are likely to be awarded high marks.

5. Candidates who present their answers strongly and effectively, with appropriate paragraphing or subheadings, as well as a beginning, middle and conclusion to their answers, are also likely to score well in the examination.

Some reasons for failing the written examination

1. *Not answering the question set (see above)*: It is not uncommon for examination students to ignore questions on the paper that they do not like and to answer the question that they would like to have been set or been asked. However well these 'questions' are answered, they will receive few if any marks.

2. *Not presenting the answer in the format required*: For Section A in particular, it is important that the answer is presented in the required format, such as a briefing paper or draft talk. Practising answering previous examination questions should help here, and if students are unsure as to how to present in a particular format they should consult their tutor well before the examination.

3. *Ignoring part of the question*: Another common reason for failing the written examination is where candidates only answer part of the question set. They drop marks by doing this. This may be because candidates cannot answer this part of the question, because they are running out of time, or because they simply

forget to complete the answer. But failing to answer the whole question results in candidates losing marks in that question.

4. *Factual errors*: Where there are factual errors, candidates are likely to fail that question. Normally this is because they lack underpinning knowledge in the field of study, which again will lose candidates marks.

5. *Responses that are too brief*: Shortened answers generally reveal that candidates lack sufficient knowledge in the field to provide a convincing answer. Again this results in fewer marks being awarded than would have been the case with normal-length answers. Individuals able to write extensively on a topic are much more likely to gain higher marks than are those who cannot do this.

6. *Failure to justify their answers*: A key attribute of M-level answers is the presentation of solid, convincing justifications to the questions put. Another reason that candidates lose marks in questions is failure to justify their answers effectively, when asked to do so.

7. *Repeating the same point in an answer*: A common fault of weak examination scripts, especially in Section B questions, is when asked for 'up to five factors', for example, for candidates to repeat the same point more than once, using different language. The key here is for candidates to think widely around the topic and to draw on knowledge gained across the standards in order to provide an effective response.

8. *Injudicious use of 'bullet points'*: Injudicious use of bullet points, especially in Section B answers, sometimes results in lack of coherence in answers. In these cases, candidates often fail to make effective links between the constituent parts of the question being answered, and thereby fail to develop an effective argument to illustrate their answers.

Some final thoughts on the examination

Students should 'aim high', that is, rather than aiming for a pass (50 per cent) they should set themselves the personal goal of attainng an examination mark of at least 60 per cent. Students who aim for just a pass face the danger of failing if things do not go quite to plan on the day. In terms of borderline pass/marginal fail candidates, the key question that the examiners will ask in reaching a decision will be whether the candidate is worthy of practising in the professional field of PM&D.

The previous section focused on common examination errors, but it is worth emphasising that many candidates perform well. A clear and focused revision programme combined with good exam technique will lead to success. Affirmation and visualisation are helpful tools in achieving success – affirming that the desired result will be achieved, and visualising the positive outcome.

Conclusion

The purpose of this chapter has been to outline how to prepare adequately for the examination, including how to manage one's time. Guidelines to revision were followed by advice on exam technique and a list of 'do's' and 'don'ts'.

3 EXAMINER'S INSIGHTS

Introduction

This chapter provides a commentary on the People Management
and Development (PM&D) examination paper for May 2004. As part
of their preparation, students may like to use this paper as a mock
examination, by attempting to do it in the allotted time of two hours
10 minutes. Alternatively, they may prefer just to work through the
paper, noting down the points they would make in response to the
questions set. Either way, the following chapter gives advice on how
to tackle the questions in this paper.

People Management and Development
examination paper May 2004: a commentary

Section A

Precise answers in this section of the paper mattered less than the
way in which the answer was put together. In essence, what the
examiners were looking for was relevance, evidence, structure, logic
and content in the answers. Where there was more than one part to
a question, each part had to be covered. Answers had to be justified
where necessary.

This section consisted of four questions and candidates had to
answer one question only. The questions were drawn from across
the professional standards and candidates had to give an in-depth
response to the question asked. The most popular question was
question 2, followed by questions 4 and 3. Question 1 was the least
popular question. In general, answers to the questions in this section
were satisfactory. As indicated above, where there was more than
one part to a question, candidates were expected to cover all of them
and to provide a justification of their response where required.

Question I

Your chief executive officer (CEO) has heard about the research literature on the 'resource-based' view (RBV) of the firm but does not fully understand what it means. He has asked you to draft a briefing paper explaining the meaning of the term and its relationship to sustained competitive advantage. He is particularly interested in how the RBV of the firm can be linked to people management and development issues within an organisation. Write your paper making sure that you cover all these issues.

In this question, candidates were asked to write a briefing paper about the 'resource-based' view of the firm and its relationship to sustained competitive advantage. The paper was to be particularly linked with how the resource-based view (RBV) of the firm can be related to PM&D issues. Basically the RBV points out that it is the range of resources, including human resources, that gives each organisation its unique character, and this may lead to differences in competitive performance across an industry. Drawing on Penrose's classical theory of the firm, writers such as Barney argue that organisations obtain sustained competitive advantage by implementing strategies that exploit their internal strengths, through responding to environmental opportunities, while neutralising external threats and avoiding internal weaknesses. The potential for sustained competitive advantage requires four specific attributes – value, rarity, imperfect imitability and lack of substitutes. In applying resource-based ideas to human resources, Wright and others argue that human resources are valuable to the extent that there is heterogeneity in the supply and demand for labour that can make differences in organisations. Human resources are rare because it is not unusual for organisations to experience skill shortages in specific areas. In terms of imitability, human resources are potentially mobile but there are substantial transaction costs in moving from one organisation to another. Imperfect mobility results in the value of human resources being accrued by the firm employing them. Human resources are seen as non-substitutable because they have the potential not to become obsolete. It is concluded that the contribution of

human resources to competitive advantage is just as significant a
that of other resources of the firm.

This was the least popular question in Section A but some candi
dates managed to tackle it quite well. Better answers outlined the key
elements of the RBV of the firm, referenced Barney and were able to
demonstrate the specific contribution of HR. Weaker candidates were
able to outline the key features of this approach but their integration
with HR practices was weak. Indeed many candidates explained the
concept in relation to resources generally rather than to their applica
tion to HR. This made their answers rather disjointed. A small number
of weak candidates attempted this question without appearing to
understand the RBV of the firm. They wrote generally about 'good
HR practice and how people are valuable assets in organisations. The
format of some of the 'briefing papers' presented was very poor, so
that their content would not have impressed their chief executives
who were their target audience, let alone have informed them.

Question 2

> You have been asked to write an article for the business supple
> ment of the local newspaper, which is running a series looking
> at contemporary management practices in firms in you
> geographical area. The title of this proposed article i
> 'Outsourcing people management and development activities
> when to do it and why'. Draft this article bearing in mind you
> target audience and their likely knowledge about people
> management and development activities. Justify you
> response.

This question required candidates to write an article for a local news
paper on 'outsourcing HR activities: when to do it and why' and to
justify their response. Candidates needed to provide some indication
of the sorts of areas where HR activities can be outsourced. These
include recruitment and selection, executive search, outplacement
training and development, and legal services. The reasons for
outsourcing personnel and development activities include insufficien
in-house expertise to deal with a particular project/situation, in some
cases external consultants cost less than in-house sources (despite
higher initial costs), management feels the need for an independent,

expert opinion not available internally, and consultants can help facilitate change. Justification for outsourcing includes using the expertise of consultants, cost and value for money, reputation and professional standing.

Responses to these questions were generally good. Good answers related well to the sorts of area to be outsourced, the reasons for deciding to do so and they included sound justifications. Good candidates were able to discuss the benefits and drawbacks of outsourcing and the types of practice likely to be outsourced, although other candidates were less confident in addressing the 'when' part of the question. Some candidates provided examples from their own organisations. Weaker candidates tended not to focus on the question set but to say all they knew about outsourcing, as well as not distinguishing between outsourcing routine administration and other major HR activities. Better answers adopted a journalistic style of writing but few demonstrated much awareness of the potential audience or provided a clear rationale for their content. Overall, there was little evidence of awareness of research on this topic and there were few academic research references. Weaker answers were unable to explain what the critical factors were in producing the conditions under which organisations would outsource HR activities.

Question 3

> Critically review learning and development strategies in your organisation in terms of the impact that they have on organisational performance and staff motivation. Indicate ways in which these strategies can be improved. In your response, take account of research in this area.

In this question, candidates were asked to critically review learning and development strategies in their organisations in terms of the impact they have on organisational performance and staff motivation. The question required candidates to make recommendations how these strategies might be redesigned so as to improve performance and staff motivation. Good responses to this question would suggest that learning and development in organisations is often routine, operational and lacks strategic vision. It was expected that candidates would draw on the literature indicating how 'people' are now viewed as the key to more productive, efficient organisations. How people are managed and how staff are developed have major impacts on quality of product/service, customer service, organisational flexibility and business costs. Effective learning and development is no longer aimed at teaching traditional skills, but at helping people how to learn and to encourage them to become lifelong learners. It could also be argued that continuous learning and development for all employees is a necessary condition for improving organisational performance and is an important element of best practice HRM. Issues relating to learning organisations or employee development and assessment programmes could be explored too.

There were some good answers but there were more weak ones than good ones. A major omission in them was not providing a critical review of learning and development within candidates' organisations. Answers on the whole tended to be descriptive, rather than analytic. Although some candidates provided explanations of the kinds of training conducted in their organisations, there was little discussion on its effectiveness and therefore on how it might be improved. A further major weakness was the focus as 'training' as opposed to learning and development. Very few answers commented on the concept of continuous learning and development and its relationship with organisational performance. Poor answers also tended to provide an account of training initiatives aimed at developing traditional skills, while neglecting the need for training people how to learn. This general weakness of describing training interventions, rather than reviewing underlying strategy, meant that linkages with performance and motivation were not generally well done.

In other cases, candidates were generally able to provide some detail about training and development practices in their own organisations but their focus tended to be operational, not strategic. Authors cited were drawn from Kolb, Honey and Mumford, and Reid and Barrington. Most answers were able to make some evaluation of the impact of learning and development on motivation but less so on organisational performance.

Question 4

The local college of further and higher education has asked you to give a short presentation to a small group of business studies students on the advantages and disadvantages of performance related pay (PRP) in organisations. Using research findings on PRP, outline what you would say in the presentation. Justify your response.

This question asked candidates to give a short presentation on the advantages and disadvantages of performance-related pay (PRP) in organisations. A definition of the term needed to be provided so that the advantages of PRP could be explored. PRP aims to motivate people and improve individual and organisational performance, act as a lever for change and encourage line managers to see objective setting as part of their managerial activities. PRP also delivers a message that performance is important and that good performance is rewarded. PRP links reward to achieved results, helps the organisation attract and retain people and rewards achievement. However, PRP can also fail to motivate where allocation of rewards is perceived to be unfair or inappropriate. Other disadvantages of PRP include difficulties associated with appraisal, difficulties of formulating objectives, risks of bias or perceived bias by appraisers, its inevitable inflationary tendency and potentially high administration costs. They also include its dubious impact on performance, problems associated with focusing on the individual and the difficulties of organising and delivering the necessary managerial commitment. It also claimed that PRP stimulates high expectations, which cannot always be satisfied.

Surprisingly, given the amount that has been written about PRP, this was not a particularly popular question, while some candidates seemed unsure of the precise meaning of the term. Relatively few answers began with a sound definition or examples of the various forms PRP can take. A small number of answers focused on payment by results (PBR). Better answers did well in linking PRP with objective setting, performance appraisal and evaluating performance. These answers also provided a balanced view of PRP and some rationale for the content of the presentation in relation to the audience. On the other hand, some candidates spent too much time presenting the talk verbatim, instead of outlining its content. There is still a tendency for candidates to have a very positive view of PRP and its motivational impact, even while citing studies of PRP, such as in the Inland Revenue, that are more critical of it. The main author referred to was Armstrong (1999), but in general wider reading of research in this area was needed. Weaker candidates tended to write a lot about PRP that was not asked for in the question.

Section B

In this section, candidates had to answer seven out of the 10 questions on the examination paper. These questions drew from across the professional standards.

Question 1

> Making sure that you take account of research evidence in the field, examine why trade union membership has declined during the past two decades.

In this question, candidates were asked to examine why trade union membership has declined during the past two decades, making sure that they took account of research evidence in the field. A number of factors have been identified as the reasons for trade union membership decline in recent years. These include the changing structure of employment (that is, from manufacturing to service industries), decline in numbers of large units of employment, lower union density in new areas of employment, contraction of manual occupations and increases in non-manual ones. Other reasons are the rise in numbers of small (non-union) firms, increases in the numbers of new workplaces with no tradition of trade unions, the rise of individualism in society and decline of collectivist values. Much of this is evidenced by the *Workplace Employee Relations Surveys, 1984–98*.

This was not, in many cases, a well-answered question. Poor answers tended to concentrate on the Thatcher/Major years and legal factors affecting trade unions rather than considering some of the more recent trends outlined above. Given that a few explanatory bullet points could have achieved a pass grade, this was a disappointing set of answers, with many candidates simply focusing on Thatcher/Major governments, sometimes with incorrect dates, and without really explaining how legislation had led to a decline in membership. Those candidates who passed, however, were able to list a number of factors including legislation, structural shift, changing employee attitudes and size of employment unit. Nevertheless, there was a tendency to make sweeping generalisations, such as 'no one needs unions any more' and 'the days of trade unions are over'. There was also little awareness that some parts of the public sector are still quite heavily unionised.

Question 2

> On what grounds would you argue that the people management and development function should take on the role as a 'business partner' in organisations?

This question asked candidates on what grounds they would argue that the people management and development function should take on the role as a 'business partner' in organisations. Writers such as Ulrich have championed the business partner role of the PM&D function. Within this framework, the HR function is seen as making a more significant contribution to the management of people, compared with traditional personnel management. Helping senior management implement change management practices facilitates this, and the business partner role is viewed as helping achieve and sustain high levels of organisational performance. The case for the business partner role also rests on HR acting in partnership with senior managers to ensure that strategy is developed and put into practical effect. In the business partner role, the HR function also helps create the systems/processes making organisations work effectively.

The majority of students were able to relate the business partner role to Ulrich's model but they had more trouble articulating why it might be advantageous. Some answers simply described the various elements of the model. Other candidates showed a reasonable understanding of Ulrich's work and presented a good case for adopting the business partner role, but the reasoning was limited to the overarching premise that HR in being more strategic makes a better contribution to organisational performance. More comment was needed on the initiatives that HR might adopt to bring this about. On the other hand, for weaker candidates, the business partner concept was obviously an alien concept. One candidate, for example, discussed how the HR function might have more freedom, if it formed a separate 'partnership' outside the organisation.

Question 3

Identify some major barriers likely to prevent vertical integration of human resources (HR) and business strategy being implemented within organisations. Discuss the extent to which these barriers apply in your organisation.

In this question, candidates were asked to identify some of the major barriers likely to prevent vertical integration of human resources (HR) and business strategy within organisations. They then had to discuss the extent to which these barriers applied in their own organisations. The evidence indicates that the major barriers to strategy implementation in organisations include managers and supervisors regarding themselves as separate from senior management, work overload among line managers and supervisors, and lack of training for line managers and supervisors. Other factors are desire on the part of supervisors for flexibility and inadvertent rule-breaking by managers, because managers are unaware that they are not following (or are breaking) organisational rules.

Better answers defined vertical integration, listed a range of potential barriers to it, and related these to these candidates' organisations. Theoretical aspects of the topic were well integrated into the better answers, but poor answers tended not to consider the organisational setting, or to provide an answer with sufficient reference to candidates' own organisations. Some candidates, while only offering one or two barriers to effective vertical integration, were able to show convincingly how these related to their own organisations. Weaker candidates were only able to mention poor communication as a barrier and the fact that line managers never listen, and added to this the suggestion that HR was in no way to blame for the barriers existing. Other weaker answers either demonstrated little knowledge of vertical integration or provided a general 'wish list' with no analysis, again with no reference to candidates' own organisations.

Question 4

Drawing on recent research, explain and review what is meant by the term 'best practice' people management and development.

This question asked candidates to explain and review the meaning of the term 'best-practice' PM&D, drawing on recent research. Best-practice PM&D, called sometimes 'high-commitment' HRM or 'high-performance work systems', is normally associated with HR practices such as employment security and internal promotion, selective hiring, sophisticated selection, extensive training, and learning and development. It is also associated with employee involvement and voice, self-managed teams and team working, high compensation contingent on performance, reduction of status differences and workplace harmonisation. The hypothesis is that particular sets of HR practices can and do improve organisational performance.

This was one of the better sets of answers in this section of the paper. It was an area that seemed to have been well covered in many centres. Most candidates were able to quote Pfeffer and to list the characteristics of high-performance work systems. In the better answers, there was some thoughtful reflection whether all these characteristics of best-practice HRM needed to be in place at the same time, if a high-performing work organisation is the aim.

The vast majority of students were aware of Pfeffer and his seven practices. Listing them with some analysis was sufficient to pass, but better answers also included more detailed discussion of their impact on organisational performance. The strongest answers cited additional studies such as those of Purcell, Guest and Huselid. These candidates also outlined some of the criticisms of best-practice claims.

Weaker candidates only listed the characteristics of best practice, without explaining them in any way. Some weak answers were merely descriptive. Others consisted of a series of non-explained bullet points, which gained few marks at M-level standard.

Question 5

Specify some of the main criticisms that line managers make about people management and development professionals. How would you respond to these criticisms?

This relatively straightforward question asked candidates to specify some of the main criticisms that line managers make about PM&D

professionals, and how they would respond to these criticisms. Research shows that line managers direct a number of criticisms at PM&D professionals. These include that HR people are out of touch with commercial realities and unable to understand business, HR constrains the autonomy of managers to take decisions, HR managers are unresponsive and slow to act, and HR practitioners promote policies that are difficult to put into effect. In order to support line managers, HR strategies need to be made up of issues that can be operationalised by line managers. Also HR can provide opportunities for line managers to work in project groups within their organisations. HR professionals, in turn, can work with line managers at the point of delivery and encourage the development of managers, so that they can contribute to strategic change.

This was a popular question and most candidates were able to identify the criticisms, but many were less able to articulate reasoned responses to them. With the majority of candidates able to list a number of criticisms (such as too slow to respond, out of touch with business reality and so on), responses to these criticisms fell into two main categories. The first showed how HR could work more closely with line managers to counter the criticisms. The second argued that managers do not really understand the function. The better answers were quite persuasive, whereas weaker ones tended to be very dismissive of management attitudes and seemed to assume that line managers 'will eventually see the light'. Some weaker candidates resorted to the bland suggestion that 'better communication' was the answer to these problems.

Question 6

> Identify up to three principal sorts of measures that are used in assessing the contribution of the people management and development function to improved organisational performance. How could these be applied in your organisation?

This question asked candidates to identify up to three principal sorts of measures that are used in assessing the contribution of the people management and development function to improved organisational performance and how could these be applied in their own organisations. What the examiners were looking for was some appreciation of the fact that measuring the contribution of the PM&D function to improved organisation performance is difficult to do for a number of reasons. These include lack of easily quantifiable outputs from PM&D and the hidden role of PM&D specialists. However, the sorts of indicators that might be used in doing this are benchmarking against HR functions elsewhere, service-level agreements and ratios of HR costs to other organisational factors.

In general candidates did not answer this question very effectively, and it posed problems to some candidates. A few did well by discussing benchmarking and service-level agreements, but many candidates merely pointed to using staff turnover and absence ratios as measures, without making it clear how they could be used to measure HR effectiveness and contribution to performance. Many answers were interpreted very narrowly. They failed to look at the benchmarking process, consider ratios of HR costs to other costs, or provide realistic measures showing how they related to the HR function.

Question 7

What value can organisations obtain from competency-based recruitment?

In this question, candidates were asked what value organisations obtain from competency-based recruitment. Basically, competency-based approaches to recruitment are being used to provide depth to the recruitment process and set a framework within which subsequent HR practices such as performance management, training and development, pay and grading can be linked. Competencies also relate behaviour to specific performance outcomes rather than with general statements such as 'disposition', 'interests outside work' and so on. They exclude behavioural measures that are not central to effective performance at a particular workplace.

Although there were some good answers to this question, with candidates generally able to list the key features of competency-based recruitment, and to describe a range of problems arising from this, many answers were vague and lacked substance, particularly regarding the potential problems. The better answers defined competencies and showed how competency-based recruitment avoided some of the pitfalls of more traditional job-based

approaches. Weaker answers tended to discuss interviewing generally but without focusing on the specific features of a competency-
based approach.

Many other answers were very limited in terms of demonstrating
knowledge and understanding of this topic. These answers reflected
uncertainty about competency-based recruitment and how it differs
from traditional approaches. Some of these answers pointed to benefits for organisations that were credible, but few actually mentioned
any benefits, refinements or enhancements to the recruitment
process and the integrity of the PM&D function in the process. Some
of the weakest responses merely explained 'value' in relation to a
'best' method and went little beyond this.

Question 8

> What are the main features of modern apprenticeships? Review
> some of the problems in implementing such apprenticeships.

This question asked candidates to identify the main features of
modern apprenticeships and to review some of the problems in
implementing them. Modern apprenticeships comprise a number
of features. They alternate work with on-the-job and off-the-job
training. Skills sector councils design appropriate frameworks to
be supplemented to meet local need, and there is no longer a time-
served element. They are open to those aged 16–24, key skills form
part of the scheme, and it is possible to progress to further or
higher education. Some problems in implementing modern
apprenticeships include variability between sectors, concern about
the NVQ framework and inadequate demand by employers. There
are also young people opting for academic studies rather than
vocational ones. Other concerns are that the number of apprentices
training is not rising, and the majority of apprenticeships are
concentrated in traditional sectors. There are also problems of
equality issues and problems in relation to the quality of trainers
and assessors.

Although there were some good answers to this question, candidates were frequently able to list the key features and describe a
range of problems, but weaker answers lacked substance, particularly concerning the potential problems. Good answers focused well

on the appropriate features of modern apprentices but they did not deal with the problems very effectively. Poor answers in some cases simply related to traditional apprenticeship characteristics. More generally, answers were limited in their knowledge and understanding. Many answers focused on rather parochial issues such as the trainee and trainer not getting on. Not many answers were able to discuss broader issues such as concern in some sectors regarding the NVQ framework.

Question 9

Explain the principles underpinning the term 'partnership agreement' between an employer and a trade union. What evidence is there to show that both partners gain from such agreements?

In this question, candidates were asked to explain the principles underpinning the term 'partnership agreement' between an employer and a trade union, and to discuss the evidence showing that both partners gain from such agreements. In essence, a partnership agreement aims to replace adversarial collective bargaining between employers and unions with a more co-operative, positive-sum relationship of mutuality. Partnership agreements have a number of features including single status for all employees, co-operation between the parties, and some kind of mutually acceptable pay review formula. Employers gain conflict-free employee relations, flexible employment practices and a working environment incorporating higher trust between employer and union, and management and employees. Unions gain a stable recognition agreement, full involvement as a representative body within the organisation, and security of employment for their members. Evidence for these developments comes from both case studies and the activities of bodies such as the Involvement and Participation Association.

Surprisingly few candidates attempted this question, and those who did failed to do justice to it. Their underpinning knowledge in this area was very limited. Many answers were responses to issues about collective bargaining and collective agreements in general, not to partnership in particular. Other responses appeared to relate to recognition in general, rather than to the specific nature of partnership agreements.

Better answers raised issues such as the move away from adversarial employee relations and issues of trust and involvement, while weaker ones showed confusion over the basic concept of partnership. Some answers, for example, contained nebulous, prescriptive and idealistic discussions relating to improved communications but failed to demonstrate how this might be achieved in practice.

Question 10

> Provide examples of non-financial rewards in your organisation. How could you justify their contribution to employee motivation and employee commitment?

This question asked candidates to provide examples of non-financial rewards in their organisations and to justify their contribution to employee motivation and employee commitment. The rationale for it was that it has long been recognised that higher pay, more benefits and new status symbols alone do not motivate employees, and that it is important to consider the role that non-financial rewards, such as recognition and feedback by employers/managers and involvement, autonomy and responsibility for employees, have on employee motivation. Examples of non-financial rewards include praise for good work done, training employees to participate in suggestion schemes, making worthwhile awards to staff, providing prizes and giving day trips to organisations. Other non-financial rewards include providing employees with the opportunity to satisfy their needs for involvement, autonomy and responsibility. This is done through job redesign, job rotation, job enlargement, job enrichment, autonomous work groups and team working.

Most candidates were able to identify some non-financial rewards, although some talked about non-salary/wage issues rather than non-financial rewards. Links to motivation and commitment were not particularly well done, with most candidates simply asserting that non-financial rewards will improve these features. Better answers discussed the psychological issues associated with motivation and commitment, and quoted Hackman and Oldham and Herzberg knowledgeably. They also gave credible organisational examples. The very weak answers showed lack of understanding of non-financial rewards and quoted dubious examples such as company cars, private medical health care and so on. Other answers contained comments relating to praise and recognition but were not supported by convincing arguments relating to employee motivation. To claim that labour turnover has been reduced or that employees appear 'happier' following some new initiative was regarded as inadequate.

Better answers identified a range of non-financial benefits and included reference to relevant research, and some even referred to Guest and his work on the psychological contract. A number of students did not score well on this question as they confused non-financial and financial benefits, by focusing on pensions, sick pay, holiday pay and company cars.

General observations

Based on the experience of this diet of examinations and previous ones, some centres and their candidates have upgraded their standards and have made an effective transition from the PQS to the PDS. There is good evidence in these cases of student reading, ability to relate this knowledge to the questions set, and ability to refer to research evidence and apply it correctly. Overall, the scripts this year contained more references to academic material than PQS scripts did. However, the references are often to CIPD textbooks rather than to journal articles or primary research studies.

On the other hand, weaker candidates seem to be taking time to adjust to the new standards. These candidates have not really grasped relevant theory or read current research findings, and they continue to make generalised assertions about concepts such as 'business partner', 'thinking performer', 'best practice', 'vertical integration', 'improved organisational performance' and so on, without necessarily understanding the concepts and relating them to research and practice in the field of PM&D.

Another major weakness of these poor-quality examination scripts is their lack of any critical analysis or systematic review. These candidates merely describe or outline a concept or process and then fail to develop it and address the question set. These scripts tend to be unreflective, with little evaluation, and they have a weak grasp of underpinning knowledge, understanding and evidence.

This is linked with something else noted in other diets of the PDS examinations. This is an over-reliance on the use of bullet points by weaker candidates. These candidates tend to merely list 'points' thought to be relevant to the question, then fail to build on these points and elaborate them in developing their answers. Such an approach to answering questions set at M-level standard does not provide adequate explanation of the argument, effects or issues being raised. It is to be avoided, if these candidates seek to achieve a pass standard.

Section B generally continues to cause more difficulties for candidates than Section A does. This may indicate that the breadth of topics, despite the choice given, provides a greater challenge to candidates than the in-depth questions in Section A. There is a common error of many candidates spending too much time in answering the Section A question, leaving them insufficient time to provide detailed answers to Section B questions. In some cases, candidates wrote more in their Section A answer than in all the questions answered in Section B. There also remain a substantial number of candidates who are not properly prepared for taking the examinations and do not have a reasonable chance of achieving a pass standard. These candidates failed both Section A and Section B.

Another weakness of some candidates in this examination diet was not providing answers in the format required by the questions set (for example, a 'review', 'paper', 'article' or 'report'). Such candidates also fail to direct their answers at their target audience (for instance, chief executive, a group of students or a newspaper readership). Even well-informed candidates fail to gain marks, if they do not answer the question in the format requested or direct their material at the audience to which they are supposed to be communicating.

Conclusion

This chapter has provided a commentary on the May 2004 People Management and Development examination paper. Some indication of what was required in tackling questions in Section A and Section B of the paper has also been given.

SECTION 3

EXAMINATION PRACTICE AND FEEDBACK

4 EXAMINATION QUESTIONS AND FEEDBACK

In the first part of this chapter, examples of answers to some of the questions in the May 2004 examination paper are given. In the second part, a selection of questions from previous examination questions is outlined, together with feedback and advice.

May 2004 examination questions and feedback

This part of the chapter provides examples of some of the responses given to the questions in the May 2004 examination paper. They are taken from different sources and are indicative of the standard needed to achieve a pass level in this examination. If you have written answers or answer plans to any of these questions you will find it useful to compare what you have written with the feedback provided here. This should help identify any gaps in your knowledge or areas for improvement.

However, no model answers are provided and the examples given here are not the only ways in which the answers could have been drafted. This is because there is likely to be a range of possible responses to each question rather than a definitive 'right' or 'wrong' answer. The examples provided here have been selected because they are acceptable answers to the questions set. To repeat, they are not definitive and some may even contain minor errors or omissions.

This is not to say that 'anything goes'. Answers must be relevant. They must clearly address the question asked, show knowledge and understanding of the subject matter (including current research and trends), demonstrate business applicability, and be clearly justified and presented. In addition, many questions require answers that make reference to an organisation, which the candidate can specify, so each answer will be distinctive. Where there are parts to questions, each part must be answered.

It is also important that candidates write to the brief set in each questions, such as a 'briefing paper', 'newspaper article', a 'student debate', a 'review' of an internal PM&D system, a 'report to the chief executive', a 'reply to an e-mail' and so on. In other words, candidate responses need to be addressed to the appropriate audience and to the context in which the question is set. Unless they do so, they are not approaching the question in the correct manner.

In this set of examples, there is one example of an examination answer from one question in Section A of the paper. In Section B selected examples from all 10 questions are provided. In each case the question is stated, the indicative content is specified, an acceptable response is provided (as an example), and further guidance suggested.

Section A

Question 2

You have been asked to write an article for the business supplement of the local newspaper which is running a series looking at contemporary management practices in firms in your geographical area. The title of this proposed article is 'Outsourcing people management and development activities: when to do it and why'. Draft this article bearing in mind your target audience and their likely knowledge about people management and development activities. Justify your response.

Indicators covered

Indicative content 3.5.

Example of an acceptable response

The outsourcing of activities relating to the management and development of people has been an increasing trend for some years. Outsourcing of people management and development (PM&D) activities is when a firm decides to have these activities performed by external companies or consultants. The sorts of activities that might be outsourced include recruitment and selection, training and development, redundancy and outplacement support, computerised HR systems, payroll, legal issues, management development, specialist projects such as staff surveys and some administrative functions. This list is neither exclusive nor exhaustive but it captures the sorts of HR practices that can be outsourced.

In some instances, entire HR services are outsourced. In others, only some activities are, with the rest remaining within the organisation. The external sources to be drawn upon include specialist consultancies, groups of HR consultants and self-employed HR professionals. Research by Torrington *et al* (2001) suggests that the main activities outsourced are training and development and recruitment and selection, whereas employee relations and communication are less likely to be outsourced.

When to outsource

The timing of outsourcing decisions is critical. In the case of BP's decision to outsource, the decision was based on the assumption that BP needed to integrate its HR activity. It had recently acquired a sister company and, as such, had a multitude of different HR practices and activities to co-ordinate. Its desire to standardise and integrate these services led to its decision to outsource. Since the decision was HR and IT led and not business led, this created dissatisfaction within the organisation and the project was subsequently put on hold.

As well as being a way to integrate HR activities, outsourcing is also used when cost reduction is a priority. Many organisations reaching their 'maturity' stage look to outsourcing as a way to reduce costs, through cutting back the HR function and the economies of scale that can be offered by using external providers of PM&D activity. Organisations providing outsourcing are often part of a shared service that provides the same services to a number of different organisations, thus creating economies of scale.

Why outsource?

Outsourcing is often seen as a means of providing PM&D expertise that does not exist internally. Hall and Torrington argue that using outsourcing companies improves the HR services provided. This is particularly common in the field of training and development, where expertise may not be in-house.

Outsourcing also offers the HR function a way of reducing the day-to-day tasks that absorb much of its time. This allows it to concentrate on the more strategic elements of the role. This was certainly the case at Westminster City Council in the late 1990s, when it was actively decided to outsource some of the more routine elements of the function such as payroll administration. As a consequence, HR was able to devote more of their time to value-added PM&D activities and it now works more strategically with the senior management team.

Another advantage of the decision to outsource is that members of the HR function, who were transferred to the new outsourced company, had the opportunity to learn and develop new specialist HR skills and practices.

Recent CIPD research on employment trends suggests that cost-savings have been the key driver behind outsourcing decisions. The transfer of HR operations to countries such as India where labour and overheads are low, is an increasing trend, not only in the HR area.

Some problems with outsourcing

Although outsourcing of PM&D activity is increasing, there are certain issues that need to be considered by the outsourcing organisation. First, outsourcing can lead to a loss of synergy in organisations. For example, Marchington and Wilkinson (2002) suggest that there needs to be clear communication channels between host and outsourcer and that the cultural values between the host and outsourced company are critical.

Second, another barrier is that the business must be involved in the decision to outsource PM&D activities. When BF outsourced most of its administrative HR activities a few years ago, it cost them a lot of money. However, a year later the programme was put on hold, because employees were not accepting the changes. One of their main complaints was that they missed the face-to-face interactions with HR staff.

Third, when certain activities are outsourced and others remain within the host organisation, work must take place to ensure that the activities are integrated horizontally. For example, recruitment and selection practices should be in line with and not conflict with, training and development practices.

Fourth, the host organisation must ensure that care is given to designing appropriate performance standards. It needs to make clear from the outset what its expectations are and then monitor performance. The problem is that day-to-day performance management is out of the hands of the organisation. However, if expected standards are made clear from the start, and incorporated into agreements, the organisation is well placed to take action if unacceptable performance standards arise and persist. This issue highlights the importance of trying to develop shared cultures or histories of the host organisation and the outsource providers. If the two are similar, the transition should be a smooth one.

Rigorous care and due diligence must be given to deciding which organisation to outsource to. It must provide the service/ expertise the organisation requires, have a proven track record and mirror the values such as customer satisfaction or team working of the host.

To conclude

There are a variety of reasons for outsourcing including the expertise available, cost and time savings, lack of internal resources to do the job and making better use of one's own staff. Whilst outsourcing has risen in prominence for a variety of reasons, organisations must be sure that their outsourcers are credible, that they understand the requirements of the job and that they fit in with the dominant culture of the organisation.

Some studies have indicated that outsourcing is likely to continue to be the trend, as organisations and the HR function look for ways to improve value-added. To outsource successfully, therefore, organisations need to know what it is, when to do it and why.

Justification

This article is not overly inundated with HR 'jargon'. It is written clearly and targeted at the relevant readership. A working definition of outsourcing is provided and use of appropriate examples and cases is made. The pros and cons of outsourcing are considered, as well as clear indicators of 'when' and 'why' it is used. Barriers to the success or not of outsourcing are provided so as to give a balanced view of the topic.

Further guidance: See Chapter 3, Section A, Question 2.

Section B

Question 1

Making sure that you take account of research evidence in the field, examine why trade union membership has declined during the past two decades.

Indicators covered

Indicative content 1.3.

Example of an acceptable response

There are several reasons why trade unions membership has declined during the past two decades. This is due to economic, political, social and legal reasons.

There have been large sectoral shifts in the employment environment in recent years, including a decline in traditional manufacturing and extractive industries, which were highly unionised. This has been accompanied by a growth in service industries that are less unionised.

An increase in flexible working has led to more women working (45 per cent in 2000) and many of them are part-time workers in service industries, where there is little tradition of union activity. Research from the WERS survey 1998 backs up this evidence of decline in union membership, by providing reasons for it.

Another key reason is political and legal. Legislation by Conservative governments between 1979 and 1997 led to a marginalising of union power. Union recognition was reduced through legislation and the right to strike was made more difficult. Similarly privatisation of parts of the public sector, which is traditionally a stronghold of union membership, has resulted in a decline in membership.

Further, a shift from collectivism to individualism in the political/social arena has also seen a reduction in union membership; as individuals became incentivised by performance related, profit related pay and personalised benefits.

Finally, growth in the number of new, non-unionised firms

has also weakened trade union membership during this period.

Further guidance: See Chapter 3, Section B, Question 1.

Question 2

On what grounds would you argue that the people management and development function should take on the role as a 'business partner' in organisations?

Indicators covered

Indicative content 2.2.

Example of an acceptable response

Ulrich identified the business partner role in his outline of the four roles of the HR function. He argued, first, that HR should work alongside the management team to ensure that strategy is implemented and integrated effectively within the organisation. Second, the business partner role has evolved from the changes that have taken place within the field and these have been in response to the needs of organisations.

In the increasingly competitive economic environment, organisations need to remain ahead of their competitors and one way of creating competitive advantage is for organisations to ensure that the firm is making the most of its resources, including its human resources.

The business partner role allows HR practitioners to become fully embedded within the organisation, thus enabling them to participate in the organisation's business and strategic decision-making.

In adopting the business partner role, HR will be taken more seriously by being integrated into organisational strategy, with vertical and horizontal integration being more likely to happen. This means that HR strategy and business strategy are more likely to run alongside each other and be less likely to conflict.

Because of this, people management issues will be taken

more seriously within the organisation and the PM&D function can demonstrate its contribution to competitive advantage.

Further guidance: See Chapter 3, Section B, Question 2.

Question 3

Identify some major barriers likely to prevent vertical integration of human resources (HR) and business strategy being implemented within organisations. Discuss the extent to which these barriers apply in your organisation.

Indicators covered

Indicative content 3.2.

Example of an acceptable response

Vertical integration between business strategy and HR strategy can be hindered by a number of factors. First, as Brewster *et al* have pointed out espoused strategy and operational strategy may be in conflict. Espoused strategy is the general direction that senior management is leading the organisation, whilst it is lower level management who implements operational strategy during their day-to-day activities. Where these are not synchronised, there can be lack of strategy integration within the organisation.

Second, HR strategies require champions to help integrate them within the business. Champions are not always present and, to be effective, need to be committed, energetic and understanding. The conditions necessary for this may not be suitable.

Third, situations arise where managers are unaware of HR rules and policies and therefore they do not comply with what is expected of them.

Fourth, divisions between senior managers and other managers may occur. Managers may not agree with the strategies being pressed on them by top management, so they do not recognise or implement them.

Fifth, managers may lack effective training and development. Therefore they do not have the competencies and skills for implementing strategies in their part of their organisations. There may also be misunderstanding about specific strategies.

Sixth, supervisors may not like the constraints placed upon them through complying with certain strategic decisions. Therefore they do not adhere to them and they remain flexible in their roles.

Regarding the extent to which these factors are present in my organisation, a large manufacturing business, there are examples of managers not being aware of the 'rules' and it is only when something goes significantly wrong that this comes to light. Given the size of the organisation, it is easy for gaps to appear between HR and corporate strategy, since there are many separate 'integrated project teams.' In these cases, local managers prefer the flexibility to interpret strategy to their own advantage, in their own working environments.

Additionally, there is a high level of movement within the organisation and within senior management. This can result in a decline in commitment by senior management to HR strategy implementation and integration.

Further guidance: See Chapter 3, Section B, Question 3.

Question 4

Drawing on recent research, explain and review what is meant by the term 'best practice' people management and development.

Indicators covered

Indicative content 3.3.

Example of an acceptable response

The term 'best practice' people management and development (PM&D) means implementing bundles of HR policies and practices that contribute to organisational performance and effective HR management within organisations. These 'bundles' are also claimed to contribute to an organisation's competitive advantage.

Research has shown that there is a correlation between these bundles of HR practices and organisational performance. Research by Guest also shows that best-practice HRM (sometimes called high-performance work systems or high-commitment HR) has positive impacts on the psychological contract. A number of best practice PM&D activities have been identified by Pfeffer and others. These include:

- *Employment security*: this basically underpins all of the items listed below. If an organisation is unable to provide employment security, it cannot expect its employees to remain loyal and committed.
- *Internal promotion*: this is seen as a part of career development by promoting within the organisation where you know your staff. The organisation only recruits externally for lower level positions.
- *Teamwork*: This involves working in teams to achieve flexibility within the organisation.
- *Employee involvement*: this, it is claimed, makes the organisation run more effectively and efficiently because the organisation uses employee involvement processes to communicate its plans and results. If the organisation is not performing well, then employees will be able to understand why and help redress this. Employees can also question the way the organisation is doing certain tasks.
- *Selective selection*: making sure that selection decisions are based on appropriate behaviours, skills and attitudes for the job is very important. Recruiting the best staff provides competitive advantage. Training and development is important, since once they have recruited outstanding talent, firms need to retain those who have been trained to keep the organisation competitive.
- *Pay*: this should be benchmarked in relation to other similar organisations and part of it can be performance based.
- *Harmonisation*: this means harmonising conditions amongst all staff. This can include holidays, conditions, periods of notice and other benefits. This makes employees feel more valued and they can pull together more as a team.

Further guidance: See Chapter 3, Section B, Question 4.

Question 5

Specify some of the main criticisms that line managers make about people management and development professionals. How would you respond to these criticisms?

Indicators covered

Indicative content 3.4.

Example of an acceptable response

Some of the main criticisms that line managers make about PM&D professionals are:

- They don't understand the business.
- They pass on HR work to them such as performance management, attendance monitoring, probation reviews, disciplinary and grievance cases.
- They don't understand that business priorities come first over HR policies.

As Legge has said, HR specialists are often caught in a vicious circle. Either they are too interventionist or not interventionist enough.

To respond to these criticisms, it is necessary to market the HR function and outline its many roles. For example, HR specialists need to establish their reputation and build up effective relationships with line managers.

They also need to be innovative and creative in ideas so that they can provide workable HR solutions for line managers. Problem solving and interpersonal skills are important here.

Forging alliances or partnerships with line managers is also important. Building good working relationships with line managers is crucial, so that line managers know that they can rely on the HR department to deliver their services professionally. This includes advice, assistance, counselling and other support.

Being well informed and up to date with current knowledge, legislation and techniques in the field to help line managers manage more effectively is also important in gaining professional credibility.

Sometimes relevant education and training is necessary on both sides. Here it is important for HR people to understand the nature of their organisation's business, so as to be effective partners with line managers.

Devolving HR to line managers is a long-term education process but HR professionals need to be involved in this educative activity. Working with and developing line managers is 'good practice' and leads to better relationships with them. It is important that they feel valued and recognise the mutuality between themselves and HR specialists.

Finally, HR is the guardian of good practice. Effective HR policies and practices and good relations between HR and line managers ensure consistency and fairness across the organisation.

Further guidance: See Chapter 3, Section B, Question 5.

Question 6

Identify up to three principal sorts of measures that are used in assessing the contribution of the people management and development function to improved organisational performance. How could these be applied in your organisation?

Indicators covered

Indicative content 3.6.

Example of an acceptable response

Three sorts of measures that are used in assessing the contribution of the PM&D function to improved performance are as follows.

- *External benchmarking*: Wyatt's Human Capital Indicator is one example of an external benchmarking tool that can evaluate the effectiveness and efficiency of HR in an organisation. In the financial services company in which I work, this model means that there is a replication of the HR function in each division. This allows for internal benchmarking between divisions or external benchmarking with other large financial service companies or firms known for best practice activities and effective HR departments. Care needs to be taken to ensure that all the measures are similar and that the context is given before making direct comparisons.

- Service level agreements: these measures identify targets and performance indicators for the function, treating it as an internal supplier. These are used particularly by HR service and administration teams that have targets to meet on a regular basis, such as the time to post internal vacancies on the intranet site. These are useful since they set expectations but they can be limiting and less relevant to 'bigger picture' business strategy.
- HR ratios: cost, time and quality ratios can be related to organisational performance. At the company where I work, the cost of the HR function can be measured against revenues, while training and development spending per person can be measured against profit per person. Currently, absence and stability ratios are reported at board level. These are useful indicators. However, they are of little use in terms of aligning themselves with business objectives, as they are generally retrospective. Nevertheless, they 'speak' the appropriate financial language, thus adding some credibility to the HR function.

In conclusion, various measures can be used to assess the contribution of HR to organisational performance. It is important that these are understood and valued by the business to gain credibility and fully demonstrate that the function adds value to it.

Further guidance: See Chapter 3, Section B, Question 6.

Question 7

What value can organisations obtain from competency-based recruitment?

Indicators covered

Indicative content 4.1.

Example of an acceptable response

Competency-based recruitment involves drawing up a list of criteria relating to the competencies or behaviours of an individual rather than other factors such as academic qualifications, sex, age and experience. Competency frameworks are increasingly being used instead of outdated person specifications (such as Munro Fraser's five point plan). This is mainly due to:

- These attributes are measurable and more objective.
- It is no longer acceptable to comment on a person's personal attributes.
- The competencies provide a framework for selection and other PM&D activities such as training, performance management and rewards, thus promoting horizontal integration.

The value that organisations can get from competency-based recruitment is:

- If you know the competencies you are looking for, you can recruit internally or externally with candidates of appropriate calibre. In the FTSE 100 financial services company in which I work, graduate recruitment lists the competencies required for employment. This allows potential candidates to assess themselves against this set of competencies and this serves as a sifting process. It also reduces the number of unsuitable candidates. This in turn reduces the cost of selection and adds value to the organisation.
- Competency-based recruitment sets expectations from the beginning. Use of competencies at the recruitment stage automatically starts to build a positive psychological contract, as the process is perceived as being fair and unbiased. This may also increase candidates' motivation to do the job effectively at an early stage, thus adding value since the candidate is inducted more quickly and is more likely to perform better.
- Competencies focus on key strengths such as team working, leadership or communication skills of individuals and widen the available pool of talent from which to select suitable candidates. This approach also allows organisations to build up a workforce that reflects not only their values but also the values and make-up of other key stakeholders.

This can include a workforce with different backgrounds, perceptions and ideas.

In conclusion, competency recruitment methods filter candidates for selection. If this process is successful, it is likely that organisational performance will increase, through the attraction of competent candidates.

Further guidance: See Chapter 3, Section B, Question 7.

Question 8

What are the main features of modern apprenticeships? Review some of the problems in implementing such apprenticeships.

Indicators covered

Indicative content 4.3.

Example of an acceptable response

Modern apprenticeships are of two types: foundation modern apprenticeships that go up to level two NVQ and advanced modern apprenticeships that go up to level 3 NVQ. Modern apprenticeships are part of government's learning initiative as outlined in its white paper *21st century skills: realising our potential*. The aim of modern apprenticeships is to link on-the-job training with theoretical and advanced practical training, based at local colleges.

In my organisation, two modern apprenticeship schemes are offered, one in horticulture, the other in gardening. The scheme is open to appropriate age groups and attracts applicants from school-leavers to graduates undertaking a career change. In general, the scheme works well, with the students attending college for two-week blocks, every two to three months.

The constraints or problems arising out of these schemes are the length of the training, which is three years long, and there are some who fail to continue the training for the three-year period. The two-week college block takes apprentices out of the workforce for a significant period of time and therefore has an impact on the work teams.

There is also a requirement for assessment at the workplace and this involves time and cost in training managers to achieve their assessor's qualification. There is also the time element that needs to be taken in the workplace and developing trainees.

Our organisation, however, has found that these schemes are generally a good method of training. It also finds that students are sought for employment opportunities, both within and outside the organisation, due to the quality and type of training scheme. Similarly, the number of applicants to the scheme is high and places on it are hard won.

Further guidance: See Chapter 3, Section B, Question 8.

Question 9

Explain the principles underpinning the term 'partnership agreement' between an employer and a trade union. What evidence is there to show that both partners gain from such agreements?

Indicators covered

Indicative content 4.5.

Example of an acceptable response

The Industrial Partnership Association outlines the main principles underpinning partnership agreements (between employers and unions) as employee involvement and voice, sharing success, informing and consulting employees about business issues, and recognition of the company's need for flexibility and employee needs for job security.

With employee involvement and employee voice, the company needs to listen to employees and is able to tap into the knowledge of workers. Employees become involved within the company and they become motivated.

Sharing success means that there is an emphasis on share plans and profit sharing. This aligns company and employee goals, thus motivating employees to contribute to the firm's performance.

Information and consultation results in the unions being consulted and informed in a timely manner about forthcoming business issues, so that the best way forward (for the benefit of both parties) can be assessed.

Company flexibility and job security are provided through flexible working and longer hours being tolerated in return for job security and no compulsory redundancies.

Case study evidence shows the 'win–win' situation available for both parties. These include Tesco and some parts of manufacturing. Employers gain, for example, by 'give and take' in terms of working hours and the end of long pay bargaining sessions. Unions, in turn, gain access to company information and the promotion of union membership.

Finally, reducing industrial conflict and recognising that union membership can mean better representation and quicker decision-making is a major plus for employers. On the other side, increased union membership, secure recognition and more power and influence in the organisation are clearly advantageous to the union side. Partnerships also provide a defined role for unions.

Further guidance: See Chapter 3, Section B, Question 9.

Question 10

Provide examples of non-financial rewards in your organisation. How could you justify their contribution to employee motivation and employee commitment?

Indicators covered

Indicative content 4.8.

Example of an acceptable response

Non-financial rewards should not be neglected by organisations, as many of them just focus on financial rewards such as pay, fringe benefits and private health care schemes. All these contribute to employee motivation and employee commitment.

Although money is a key motivator, recent research by Guest has shown that other things motivate people as well. Guest's survey showed that people want a good working relationship with their manager, an opportunity to work as part of a team, an opportunity to get on and the chance of being developed at work, as well as good pay and financial rewards.

Traditional motivation theories have also demonstrated needs of self-actualisation (Maslow) by workers and expectancy theory (Vroom) has shown that people expect different things within their work environment.

In my organisation, we have a 'values award scheme'. This involves 'token' awards, where staff are given certificates and badges for living the company values, showing extra commitment or working beyond contract. This helps build motivation by improving the psychological contract between employer and employee and sustains mutual respect between the two.

Other forms of non-financial reward include regular feedback from management to workforce. One of our company's values is to praise staff rather than criticise them. This again helps develop and motivate staff through good working relationships with their managers. Recent research backs this up by showing that regular positive feedback is an important component of non-financial reward.

Other ways in which we provide non-financial reward is by allowing staff to work as part of a team in project activities. This gives them more involvement in decision-making. This ultimately helps them improve their working lives and improves their motivation and commitment.

Further guidance: See Chapter 3, Section B, Question 10.

Previous examination questions and feedback

In this section, brief feedback and advice is given on all the questions in the May 2003 paper, and a selection of questions taken from the

November 2003 and specimen examination papers. The full versions of the examination papers can be accessed on the CIPD's website.

If, as part of your revision, you have produced written answers or answer plans to these questions you will find it useful to compare what you have written to the feedback provided here in order to identify any gaps and areas for improvement.

May 2003 paper: Section A

Question 1

> Your new chief executive has asked you to prepare an internal paper outlining and evaluating how recent changes in the political, economic and legal environment have affected your organisation in terms of its people management and development policies and practices. Draft this document, by identifying the main issues, discussing them and providing any necessary background to your organisation.

In this question, candidates are asked to prepare an internal paper for their CEO evaluating how recent changes in the political, economic and legal environment have affected their organisation in terms of its PD&M polices and practices. This question gives wide scope for candidates to identify those issues most affecting their own organisations. In answering the question, it is necessary for candidates to provide an outline background to their organisation and the external environmental pressures facing it. No area of environmental change is proscribed or prescribed.

Particular changes affect specific organisations differentially. Political changes in government policy, for example, particularly affect public organisations such as the modernisation agenda in the public services, with attendant impacts on people management and development practices. Economic changes, such as changes in fiscal or monetary policy, affect demand for products or services in the private sector and hence impact on issues such as recruitment and selection, human resources planning and managing redundancy. Legal changes arising from either UK employment legislation or that of the EU, such as union recognition, the national minimum wage and family-friendly policies, similarly impact on related people management and development decisions. This question seeks an in-depth answer identifying the main issues, discussing them and analysing them in an organisational context.

Better marks will be awarded to candidates who identify a wider range of issues and how these impact on their organisations. Candidates also need to evaluate and discuss their findings. Good answers will be well balanced between the two main themes – external changes and their impact on organisations. Candidates need to demonstrate strategic awareness and critical analysis. Political, environmental and legal issues need to be discussed in terms of the impact they would have on HR issues.

Answers need to be produced in the form of an internal paper for the CEO. They need to be clearly written, coherent and provide clear explanation of points.

Question 2

The topic for the annual management debate at the local branch of the Chartered Management Institute (CMI) is 'Business is business and ethical considerations are not the responsibility of business organisations'. As a leading member of the Chartered Institute of Personnel and Development (CIPD) locally, you have been invited by the Chair of the CMI to oppose this motion. You want to give a good professional and personal impression by accepting the invitation and putting on a convincing performance at the debate. Outline the arguments that you would use and indicate how you will try to persuade the audience to support your case.

This question requires candidates to prepare for a debate at the local branch of the Chartered Management Institute. The topic is 'Business is business and ethical considerations are not the responsibility of business organisations'. Candidates are asked to oppose this motion and to outline the arguments that they would use, indicating how they would try to persuade the audience to support their case.

Responses to this question could start with an outline of what the motion stands for, namely that, in free market conditions, the only social responsibility business has is to maximise its profits and it is government's residual task to promote 'good values', if this is supported by the electorate. A major set of arguments against the motion rests on the 'stakeholder' model of business. This suggests that shareholders, employees, customers, suppliers, the community and those with a concern for the environment, all have a stake or an interest in ethical business practices. Ethicality, it is claimed, makes economic sense since an ethical business is more likely to be successful than an unethical one. This is likely to result in improved motivation of staff, better reputation/loyalty with customers and better relations with corporate stakeholders.

Ethicality make social sense too because, with government providing minimum ethical standards in terms of consumer protection, employment rights, and health and safety, many people expect businesses to go beyond minimum legal requirements. Ethicality also balances organisational interests, thus ensuring that no interest becomes dominant. Some examples of good practice in ethical behaviour by model organisations could be provided in the debate. Candidates also need to indicate how they would try to persuade their audience to support their case, in a convincing way.

Recent examples of ethical business practices need to be discussed. Clear arguments would need to be delivered in order to convince what may be a fairly critical audience. Good answers would focus on the subject matter of the debate and take the stakeholder view of the firm to argue against the motion. Clear examples of organisations that operate in a model way in terms of ethical considerations in business would be included.

Question 3

The local sixth-form college has a lunch-hour business forum for students, where invited speakers talk about 'Current business issues'. You have been asked to give a short talk, followed by a discussion, to about 40 students on the importance of the people management and development function in contributing to organisational performance. What will you say and why?

In this question, candidates are asked to give a short talk, followed by a discussion, to about 40 students on the importance of the people management and development function in contributing to organisational performance. They also have to justify their answer.

This question is prompted by the search for establishing links between effective PM&D activities and organisational performance, which is now a major research area in HRM. The debate focuses on the works of Guest and others and the role of high-commitment work practices as drivers of high performance. This debate is not without controversy but has strong support. The HR activities claimed to enhance performance include: appropriate job design, recruitment and selection, training and development, appraisal, rewards, communication, job security and harmonisation practices.

HR performance outcomes include employee competence, commitment and flexibility. Organisational performance outcomes claimed include quality of goods and services, productivity and efficiency. Candidates are expected to argue that the case justifying the HRM/performance link is based on the claim that the greater the number of HR practices employed by organisations, the higher their levels of reported productivity, quality and financial results. The more effectively these HR practices are used, the better its organisational performance.

This question therefore requires knowledge of the literature to demonstrate how these HR practices result in improved performance. Answers need to make reference to the work of scholars such as Guest and Pfeffer, the issue of HR bundles and research into the HRM–organisational performance link. This is the key element of the discussion. Good answers therefore need to make clear links to relevant research studies and supporting evidence, as well as raising the critical issues and questions surrounding this area. The arguments need to be of a suitable level and format for sixth-form college students.

Question 4

The Human Resources (HR) Director has asked you to critically review the appraisal system for a specified group of staff within your organisation. Drawing on recent research in the field, and your knowledge of other organisations, discuss how this appraisal system might be changed to improve organisational performance. Indicate what those improvements will be.

This question asks candidates to critically review the appraisal system for a specified group of staff within their own organisation. They are expected to draw on recent research in the field, their knowledge of other organisations, and discuss how this appraisal system might be changed to improve performance.

Answers need to outline these schemes, review them and assess their impact on performance. Just describing an existing staff appraisal scheme is not sufficient. Responses should also discuss some measures of performance that might link with effective staff appraisal schemes in terms of efficiency, productivity, profitability, absenteeism, turnover and so on. Candidates would also be expected to address the issue of what changes in existing schemes might improve performance in these areas. Thus they need to be able to assess and critique their organisation's approach to appraisal. Better answers would include a review of the part that appraisal plays within performance management.

In answering this question, candidates need to make reference to recent research, such as CIPD research reports, and make use of knowledge of other organisations. Clear proposals need to be made for improvement. These recommendations need to be appropriate for the circumstances. Answers need to provide more than merely a description of the appraisal process, and analyses need to be linked to theory.

May 2003 paper: Section B

Question 1

Identify the main types of flexible employment practices that have been introduced into your organisation in recent years. Explain why this has or has not happened and assess their impact on organisational effectiveness.

In this question, candidates are asked to identify the main types of flexible employment practices that have been introduced into their organisations in recent years. They also have to explain why this has or has not happened and to assess the impact on organisational effectiveness.

Some definitions of flexible employment practices are required, but with reference to candidates' own organisations. There are various ways of defining employment flexibility in terms of hours of work, contractual arrangements and working practices. A more formal framework of analysis could include numerical, functional and pay and outsourcing flexibilities, as per Atkinson. The factors leading to employment flexibilities include product and labour market pressures, government policy and globalisation of international trade. These incorporate sectoral shifts in employment from manufacturing to services, the changing gender distribution of the workforce, extended working hours to meet customer needs and employer needs to maximise use of expensive capital.

Answers to the question also need to assess the impact of flexibilities on organisational performance in the organisations of candidates, doing this by drawing on appropriate examples. All parts of the question need to be addressed, including the impact of such practices, and answers should include a discussion of the factors that have led to an increase in flexible working practices. It is useful to make reference to relevant models, such as Atkinson's, but these need to be applied to the question and not just described.

Question 2

You have been asked by the head of people management and development to undertake a salary survey of secretarial staff in your locality. Outline what you would aim to do, how you would do it and why.

This question asks candidates to undertake a salary survey of secretarial staff in their locality, outlining what they would aim to do, how they would do it and why they would do it. The key part of the question is 'a salary survey of secretarial staff in your locality' and any answer needs to be centred on this requirement.

There are several ways in which this task could be done. Basically, the aim of the research would be to get information on the salaries paid to secretarial staff from local employers in the private and public sectors, in a sensitive manner. A main method of data collection could be by contacting local employers and using either telephone interviews or short postal questionnaires for this purpose.

These would seek to provide a cost-effective way of collecting the information, which is both reliable and valid in the circumstances, and would be reported to the head of people management and development services. Better answers will consider realistic primary and secondary research options.

The question has three parts. Thus detail of the method of data collection needs to be outlined and justified against other methods in terms of reliability, cost-effectiveness and validity.

Question 3

Various researchers have identified a number of models of the human resources/people management and development function. Identify one of these models and critically assess its usefulness as a tool for understanding the complexity of the function. How does this model relate to your organisation?

In this question, candidates are asked to identify one model of the human resources/people management and development function and critically assess its usefulness as a tool for understanding the complexity of the function. They are also asked how this model related to their organisation.

A number of personnel and development/HR models could be identified, analysed and explored. These include Legge, Tyson and Fell, Storey, Monks, Shipton and McAuley, and Ulrich (see Marchington and Wilkinson (2002) for details). No model is preferred, but answers need to be related to the candidates' own organisations; thus application needs to be encompassed.

The danger with this sort of question is that candidates, instead of exploring a model and applying it to their own organisations, will merely set out the key sections of the model, describe their organisation and fail to make a link between the two. This would result in answers that are merely descriptive and should be avoided!

Question 4

Organisations are increasingly using external management consultants to undertake people management and development activities for them. Explain why this is happening and justify a list of suitable criteria by which such consultants might be selected. Give examples from your organisation where appropriate.

This question asked why organisations are increasingly using external management consultants to undertake PM&D activities within them. Candidates also have to explain why this is happening and to justify a list of suitable criteria by which such consultants might be selected, giving examples from their own organisations where appropriate.

The reasons for outsourcing personnel and development activities include insufficient in-house expertise to deal with a particular project/situation. In some cases external consultants cost less than in-house sources, and despite higher initial costs, management feels the need for an independent/expert opinion not available internally, so that it can help facilitate change. Criteria of selection include expertise, cost and value for money, reputation and a justified reason. Examples need to be provided from candidates' own organisations.

Candidates therefore need to provide a critical review of the use of consultants. Explanation and justification needs to be provided rather than mere description. Once again, the question is in three parts. These are, to repeat, outlining why use of consultants has increased, choice and justification of criteria for selection, and providing examples from their own organisations. All three parts need to be covered.

Question 5

Identify the most common forms of recruitment methods used in your organisation. Assess how far they are cost-effective.

This question asks candidates to identify the most common forms of recruitment methods used in their organisations and to assess how far they are cost-effective.

Identifying the methods used should be quite straightforward. Their cost-effectiveness also needs to be analysed. How such cost could be measured and comparisons made should be outlined, as well as the difficulties involved in this. Better answers would draw on other company data, such as the cost of staff turnover, and apply classic correlation measures on method/performance.

Question 6

Evaluate the factors leading to the growth of performance management systems in organisations. What is the evidence that such systems add value to organisations?

This question asks candidates to evaluate the factors leading to the growth of performance management systems in organisations and to review the evidence that such systems add value to organisations. The factors leading to the growth of performance management systems in organisations include increased competitive pressures putting emphasis on performance improvement, attempts to achieve clearer correlation between organisational goals and personal targets, delegation of tasks and responsibilities down organisational hierarchies, and the shift from collectivism to individualism.

Other factors include allowing specifications of individual performance standards and measures and the introduction of performance management processes in the public sector. Added value comes from more effective staff performance, better customer satisfaction and improved organisational performance. Both the external and internal factors leading to performance management systems need to be identified. Once again, all aspects of the question need to be tackled.

Question 7

Given the many criticisms of Investors in People (IiP), how can an organisation use IiP to best advantage?

Candidates are asked in this question to examine the many criticisms of Investors in People (IiP) and indicate how organisations can use IiP to best advantage.

The IiP standard provides a national framework for improving organisational performance, through a planned approach to setting and communicating corporate objectives and developing people to meet them. IiP is claimed to benefit the organisation, its employees and customers in a variety of ways. These need to be explored by candidates. Some of the concerns about IiP are the 'badging' process (that is, organisations use it to badge their current systems, not to improve training), failure to engage in best-practice training (that is, it is a paper exercise), and weak links between training and IiP. There is also the inability to demonstrate a definitive connection between IiP and profitability and failure to establish links between IiP and staff motivation.

It is important that answers address the concerns about IiP and incorporate them in answering how to get the best out of the standard. Critical analysis needs to be displayed as well as knowledge of the subject matter.

Question 8

> Critically review the role of trade union learning representatives in workplaces.

This question asks candidates to critically review the role of trade union learning representatives in workplaces. The role of trade union learning representatives includes generating demand for learning among members, advising about learning, identifying the learning needs of members, negotiating agreements incorporating learning and setting up joint training or learning committees. Other roles include working with employers to introduce and monitor initiatives that benefit members, taking joint ownership of employee development schemes and liaising with providers of training to support workplace learning. Some of the difficulties encountered include reaching a wide range of members/employees, some employer resistance where unions are recognised, and a limited role where there is no union recognition, and problems of small and medium-sized enterprises.

It is important that candidates critically review, rather than just describe the role. Better answers would include an analysis of the recent legislation and accepted practice in this area.

Question 9

> What are the major problems managing employee grievances? Drawing on evidence from your organisation, what are some of the problems in operating such a procedure? How would you overcome these problems?

In this question, candidates are asked to consider the major problems of managing employee grievances. They are required to draw on evidence from their own organisations and examine some of the problems in operating such a procedure and how they could be overcome. The objectives of an effective grievance procedure include preventing issues and disagreements between managers and staff leading to major conflict, preventing employees leaving the employer, and establishing a fair and legitimate process for determining grievances. The basic elements of a grievance procedure are that it is formal and written, agreed with employee or union representatives, linked with the procedure to avoid disputes, and issues are settled close to the point of origin. Other elements are the right of employees to be accompanied and ensuring confidentiality of the process. Problems can arise from any of the above elements.

Answers thus need to identify a sufficient number of problems and make adequate recommendations to counteract them. Candidates need to link their answer to their own organisations.

Question 10

What does research on payment by results (PBR) schemes tell us about the conditions under which PBR schemes are likely to be most effective?

This question asks candidates what research on payment by results (PBR) schemes reveals about the conditions under which PBR schemes are likely to be most effective. Basically, PBR attempts to link reward and effort so as to motivate workers. Candidates need to differentiate between individual PBR (for example, piece rates) and collective PBR (for example, group bonuses). In general, PBR is best used where technological change is slow, quality of output is not an issue, work activities can be measured accurately, standards of performance can be set, and product development is sluggish. As with all questions, it is vital to address the question asked, which includes a consideration of the conditions under which PBR is likely to be effective. Relevant research would include that of White and Druker (2000), while trends in such schemes are outlined by Millward *et al* (2000), and authors who have made reference to such research and trends include Armstrong (2001).

November 2003 and specimen paper

The following is a selection of questions taken from the Novembe:
2003 and the specimen paper.

Section A

As part of your organisation's management developmen
programme, you have been asked to give a 20-minute talk to :
group of new first line managers on 'High performance worl
systems'. Write an outline of what you would say, providin;
examples as necessary, and justify your answer.

This question asks candidates to provide an outline of what the)
would include in a talk on high-performance work systems to :
group of line managers. The question relates to those parts of th(
standards that relate to the notion of 'best practice', human capital advantage, horizontal integration, and bundles of personne
and development practices likely to enhance organisationa
performance. High-performance work systems are sometime:
referred to as best-practice HRM, high-commitment HRM o
high-involvement HRM. The components of such best-practic(
approaches have been identified by a number of studies, including those of Pfeffer, Storey, Wood, Huselid, and Guest anc
Conway. Pfeffer, for example, specifies the following: employment security and internal promotion, selective hiring anc
sophisticated selection, extensive training, learning and develop
ment, employee involvement and voice, self-managed teams anc
team working, high compensation dependent on organisationa
performance, reduction of status differences and introduction o:
harmonisation. The premise is that such high-performance worl
systems improve organisational performance.

Answers should provide an outline of such high-performanc(
work systems and examples of the components, along with discus
sion of the link to organisational performance, together with organisational examples. Consideration needs to be given to the targe'
audience, that is, the concept of high performance work system:
needs to be 'sold' to the line managers.

Your new chief executive has asked you to prepare an outline paper indicating how people management and development strategy in an organisation of your choice might be integrated with organisational strategy and thereby contribute to improved organisational performance. Draft this paper, providing any necessary background information about this organisation to justify your response.

This question is concerned with how PM&D strategy might be vertically integrated with organisational strategy within an organisation of the candidate's choice, and how this might contribute to improved organisational performance. It gives candidates an opportunity to review the business strategy of an organisation and to comment on the 'fit' between this and its people management and development activities.

In answering this question, it is essential that candidates provide sufficient information about the organisation in question in order to make a persuasive case. Where vertical integration is weak or poorly defined in this organisation, for example, candidates might suggest that achieving fit between business strategy and PM&D strategy in practice is problematic. Much depends on the contingencies of the organisation in terms of its size, structure, market position, ownership and the personalities, skills and expectations of those in top positions, as well as the credibility of PM&D professionals. However, demonstrating the potential contribution of PM&D activities to managing and improving performance through examples of appropriate resourcing, reward, relations, and learning and development policies and practices would be a useful starting point in developing an effective dialogue with the chief executive. Where vertical integration is strong, concrete examples of 'good fit' could be identified and evaluated.

The question asks candidates to provide a paper to the new chief executive, and they need to address this in an appropriate way.

You have been asked to make a presentation to a group of 30 management students at your local college of further education on 'how employee learning and development can contribute to the bottom line in organisations'. Outline the learning outcomes you want to be achieved, specify what you

> plan to say and indicate how you will make your presentation
> an interesting one for the group. Justify your answer.

This question asks candidates to outline a presentation to a group of
management students on 'how employee learning and development
can contribute to the bottom line in organisations'. It asks candidates
to identify their learning outcomes, specify what they plan to say,
indicate how they will make their presentation an interesting one and
justify their answer. The question reflects the focus in the standards on
managing learning processes for organisational success.

The argument to be presented by candidates centres on the role
that planned learning and development activities – such as courses,
events, assignments and so on – can take, and how this can be
aligned with organisational objectives and the organisation's business priorities. Such learning and development activities need to
motivate trainees and involve line managers in planning learning
and development, coaching and mentoring, as well as gaining senior
management support to promote learning in line with the dominant
corporate culture. The latter objective is more difficult to achieve,
but the advantage of this rational approach to learning and development is that it provides a useful framework for developing the
presentation in an interesting and participative way. For making the
presentation interesting, candidates could suggest that a professional PowerPoint presentation might be used, and that the presen-
ter could draw on workplace experiences (both positive and
negative) to make a more interactive presentation.

> Critically review EITHER the reward management strategies of
> your organisation OR the employee relations strategies in
> terms of impact that they have on organisational performance
> and staff motivation. In the light of this review, make appro-
> priate recommendations on how these strategies might be
> redesigned in order to improve organisational performance
> and staff motivation.

In terms of employee relations, the new standards stress effectiveness, not just knowledge of processes and functions. The involvement of line management and the value of agreed mechanisms and
procedures are also highlighted.

In terms of reward management, motivation is brought to the fore, and choosing appropriate methods of reward. Issues of harmonisation and equality are also stressed.

The question enables candidates to select either the reward strategies of their organisation or its employee relations strategy, critically review them in terms of organisational performance and motivation, and make recommendations to improve the system under discussion. Candidates need to specify and describe their existing employee relations or reward system, and explore it in terms of its impact on performance and motivation. Reward systems could be examined in terms of their impact on motivating staff, regarding contributions, and delivering equity and fairness. Care is needed to ensure that recommendations are clearly justified and are appropriate for the organisation in question.

In terms of employee relations, the central issue is the extent to which existing structures and processes – whether in a unionised, part-unionised or non-unionised environment – facilitate or fail to facilitate employee commitment and involvement. In either case, in making recommendations for change, candidates need to provide firm evidence for vertical integration of the reward or relations strategy they propose.

Section B

Evaluate how changes in the political and legal environment have affected your organisation in recent years.

This question asks candidates to evaluate how changes in the political and legal environment have affected their organisation in recent years. It draws on that aspect of the PM&D standards that refers to the political and legal frameworks in which employing organisations operate. Candidates have a wide range of choice of changes to identify and comment on. Politically, these could include a two-term Labour government, political devolution in Scotland and Wales, and developments in the European Union. Legally, this could include recent legislative developments in the areas of flexible working, family-friendly policies, discrimination and consultation. Evaluation of the identified changes needs strong emphasis in answers.

Identify and discuss one 'best-fit' model of Human Resource Management. What are some of the limitations of best-fit models?

The question asks candidates to describe and discuss one best-fit model of HRM, and identify some of the limitations of best-fit models. There are three main best-fit models of HRM: life cycle, competitive advantage and strategic configuration. Life-cycle models encompass start up, growth, maturity and decline phases. Competitive advantage models link Porter's competitive strategies (cost reduction, quality enhancement, innovation) to HR practices. Strategic configuration models seek internally consistent sets of HR practices that maximise horizontal integration and link these with strategic configurations to maximise vertical integration. The limitations of best-fit models include assumptions that it is possible to have preferred HR strategies from knowledge of business strategy or competitive prospects, that they follow traditional scientific principles, that they fail to focus on the processes involved, and that categorisation of real organisations is problematic.

Assess the research skills involved in preparing a report for your chief executive on EITHER the recruitment problems facing your organisation and how these might be addressed OR how induction training in your organisation might be improved.

The focus of this question is on research management and change skills, demonstrating the concern of the new standards to reflect the personal and professional skills needed by the PM&D professional to operate effectively in real work situations. These skills include identifying, researching, preparing and presenting a case, and communicating and team building.

The question is asking candidates to identify and assess the research skills needed in preparing a report to the candidate's chief executive on either the recruitment problems facing their organisation (and how to address them) or how induction training might be improved. It is not about recruitment problems or induction training in general taken out of context.

In this question, recruitment and induction are being used as a means of getting candidates to identify the appropriate information sources, both internal and external, and the research skills necessary to enable them to make a persuasive written report to senior management on one of these issues. In either case, the sort of research skills that might be identified includes: accessing, analysing and presenting relevant data; using statistical sources and information technology; and report writing and presentation skills.

> What ethical principles should underpin the activities of the people management and development professional? Provide examples where these principles might conflict with organisational objectives and why.

Ethics and professionalism form an important part of the PM&D Standards. This question asks candidates to examine the ethical principles underpinning the activities of PM&D professionals and asks them to give examples where these principles might conflict with organisational objectives, and why.

Here candidates need to explore the various dimensions of ethical behaviours within the PM&D function, such as compliance with the law, integrating individual and organisational goals to a common purpose, and treating individual employees fairly, consistently and in accordance with agreed rules and procedures. The assumption is that the behaviours need not normally conflict with sound business practice and organisational efficiency. Indeed, positive benefits can accrue from well-designed equal opportunity policies and the management of diversity, monitored by codes of practice and espoused ethical guidelines within organisations.

Candidates might also usefully explore some of the moral and practical issues relating to the management of people and the nature and extent of disadvantage and discrimination in relation to age, ethnic group, marital status, sex and disability. Conflicts between an organisation's ethical principles and its corporate goals can arise in a variety of ways, including poorly codified guidelines and inadequate managerial monitoring of ethical policies. Conflicts also occur where contingent management decisions are taken on purely market or financial criteria and lip service is paid by managers to basic ethical principles to ensure organisational success.

> Give examples of the people management and development activities most likely to be devolved to line managers. Discuss how the people management and development professional can ensure that line managers undertake these tasks effectively.

The new standards sharpen the focus on the line management role in organisations and partnerships between line managers and PM&D professionals, as well as the possible difficulties involved in devolution. The question asks candidates to give examples of the PM&D activities most likely to be devolved to line managers and how they can ensure that line managers carry them out effectively. The activities that could be identified include selection, appraisal, mentoring, staff development, grievance handling and discipline issues.

The central role of PM&D departments in providing the policies, procedures and systems within which devolution takes place needs to be highlighted, as well as their monitoring role in terms of consistency and even-handedness. The importance of management and development of line managers, facilitated by PM&D professionals, also needs to be explored and discussed.

Better answers will make reference to relevant studies, such as those by Hutchinson and Wood, and Torrington and Hall.

> In what circumstances are employers likely to use external people management and development consultants rather than in-house resources for advice?

The standards examine the role of consultants and outsourcing in people management, looking at the rationale for using and differentiating between consultants and the contribution they make to organisations. This question focuses on the conditions when employers are likely to ask external consultants for advice, rather than in-house sources. The factors to be taken into account include: the relative availability of in-house expertise; the relative cost advantage of external advice; speed of response to organisational needs; the opportunity provided to put contracts out to external tendering and hence get 'value for money'; and the opportunity to draw on external networks for wider professional purposes.

Identify the elements of cost-effective recruitment advertising and explain how it can contribute to effective staff selection.

The standards focus on effectiveness, cost implications and appropriateness, and these are reflected in this question. The notion of adding value is also encompassed. For this question, some measure of 'cost-effective' needs to be provided, for the purposes of comparison, and what is meant by 'effective selection'. Then the relative merits of the specialist or general press, international, national and local outlets, the Internet and word of mouth could be explored, and these linked with expected selection outcomes.

Provide examples of self-directed, group-based methods of learning and critically review their effectiveness in contributing to individual and organisational learning.

The standards include a focus on maximising skills and contributions by understanding the nature of learning and searching for a clear picture of why and how learning and development adds value for the organisation and individuals. In line with these changes, this question asks candidates to provide examples of self-directed, group-based methods of training and to review their effectiveness in contributing to individual and organisational learning. Examples that could be provided include learning sets, group-based projects, action learning and video conferencing. These demand varying degrees of monitoring and evaluation but measurement/review of their outputs in line with predetermined targets and timescales, and provision for integrating organisational and individual learning, seem the best way forward.

Explain how partnership agreements between employers and trade unions can contribute to effective employment relations in organisations.

This question relates to the contribution that partnership agreements between employers and trade unions can make to effective employee relations in organisations. A definition of partnership agreements and some indication of their variety of form and content are required. Candidates need to show awareness that there is no definitive model template of employer–union partnership agreements. However, their contribution to effective employee relations derives from their emphasis on co-operation between management and union(s), the establishment of single status for all employees, and development of mutually acceptable pay review formulae. Partnership agreements also tend to promote openness on problems and issues of mutual concern and they value good communication, consultation and negotiation. Such agreements aim to avoid disruptive workplace conflict.

> Under what circumstances is individual performance-related pay most likely to motivate employees?

Motivating staff and rewarding contribution is a main theme of the standards. This question draws on this theme and asks candidates to examine the circumstances under which individual performance-related pay is best suited to motivate employees. It contrasts with the increasing volume of literature that indicates how many employees identify with the principle of such an approach to pay, but criticise its implementation.

These critiques provide the clues where performance-related pay is likely to be more effective in motivating staff. These include: where agreed employee outputs/targets can be effectively measured; where there is a fair and respected system of staff appraisal; where a platform of base pay can be supplemented by known and specific additions to pay; where there is sufficient 'global' money for performance supplements; and where there is a legitimate system of appeal against disputed management decisions.

Conclusion

This chapter has provided some examples of acceptable responses to questions taken from Section A and Section B of the May 2004 examination. It needs to be repeated that there are no 'model' answers. Answers need to address the question set, demonstrate knowledge and understanding of the relevant standards, and respond to all parts of the question.

Questions from previous examinations have also been outlined, together with relevant feedback and advice.

SECTION 4

CONCLUSION

5 CONCLUSION

In this revision guide, the authors have given suggestions as to how to prepare for, revise for and take the People Management and Development (PM&D) examination.

It is important that the examination itself is seen as merely the final part of an ongoing process, of which revision constitutes the penultimate part. Students should familiarise themselves with the standard and associated content, which are outlined and reviewed in the first chapter of this guide, early on in their course of study. They can then refer to these on an ongoing basis throughout their studies and during the revision period.

This revision guide should be used in conjunction with the core PM&D text by Marchington and Wilkinson (2002). Additional reading can then be done around specific topic areas, and the core text provides a basis for this. Students should also keep up to date with relevant trends, articles and research reports. For each topic, relevant material can then be collected and classified. This forms a suitable basis for revision on a focused and structured basis. Material on a particular topic can then be summarised and condensed into revision notes.

Past examination questions can be attempted and answers compared with those suggested in this guide. The suggestions on examination technique should also be noted.

Few people profess to an enjoyment of examinations, but if the above process is followed, rather than being a source of trepidation, such examinations can be viewed as a positive challenge. The authors of this guide wish you every success in your People Management and Development examination.

REFERENCES

ARMSTRONG, M. (2001) *A handbook of human resource management.* 8th edn. London: Kogan Page.

ATKINSON, J. (1984) 'Manpower strategies for the flexible organisation'. *Personnel Management.* August, pp28–31.

ATKINSON, J. and MEAGER, N. (1986) 'Is flexibility a flash in the pan?' *Personnel Management.* September, pp26–31.

BRATTON, J. and GOLD, J. (2003) *Human resource management: theory and practice.* Basingstoke: Palgrave.

CHAMBERS, E. and NORTHEDGE, A. (1997) *The arts good study guide.* Milton Keynes: Open University Press.

HUSELID, M. (1995) 'The impact of human resource management practices on turnover, productivity and corporate financial performance'. *Academy of Management Journal.* Vol. 38, No. 3, pp635–672.

HUTCHINSON, S. and WOOD, S. (1995) 'The UK experience' in *Institute of Personnel and Development: Personnel and the Line.* London: IPD, pp3–42.

LEWIS, M. and SARGEANT, M. (2002) *Essentials of employment law.* 3rd edn. London: CIPD.

MARCHINGTON and WILKINSON (2002) *People management and development.* London: CIPD

MILLWARD, N., BRYSON, A. AND FORTH, J. (2000) *All change at work: British employment relations 1980–1998.* London: Routledge.

MONKS, K. (1993) 'Models of personnel management: a means of understanding the diversity of personnel practices?' *Human Resource Management Journal.* Vol. 3, No. 2, pp29–41.

PFEFFER, J. (1998) *The human equation: building profits by putting people first.* Boston: Harvard Business School Press.

TORRINGTON, D., HALL, L. and TAYLOR, S. (eds) (2001) *Human resource management.* London: FT Prentice Hall.

WHITE, G. and DRUKER, J. (eds) (2000) *Reward management: a critical text.* London: Routledge.

WOOD, S. (1999) 'Human resource management and performance', *International Journal of Management Studies.* Vol. 1, No. 4, pp367–413.

INDEX